PRAISE FOR

What Your Parents Didn't Tell You

In *What Your Parents Didn't Tell You*, Francesco Lombardo masterfully explores the emotional legacies families unknowingly pass down through generations. This book sheds light on how financial security often fails to guarantee emotional well-being, with negative emotional traditions and harmful behavioral patterns perpetuating a cycle of silent pain. Francesco unearths the subtle but powerful "ecology of beliefs" that shape family dynamics, revealing how rules and narratives become normalized, ultimately affecting future generations. Through this eye-opening work, Francesco offers a path to healing generational wounds and creating a new, positive emotional legacy. This book is a must-read for anyone seeking to break free from inherited emotional burdens and build a healthier future.

Olivier de Richoufftz, Secretary General, Family Enterprise Foundation–Switzerland

This is one of the most important books I've read on family, wealth, and legacy. Franco Lombardo gives language and structure to something many families feel but rarely understand. He shows us how emotional inheritance shapes outcomes more powerfully as

financial inheritance. This book is not about casting blame. Instead, it's focused on responsibility, awareness, and the thoughtful design of emotional governance. For anyone serious about stewarding their financial, social, and human capital today, and across generations, this is essential reading.

Mo Lidsky, Chairman and Chief Executive Officer, Prime Quadrant - Canada

As someone deeply immersed in the world of family businesses, I can wholeheartedly recommend Franco Lombardo for his exceptional guidance. He provides valuable insights with a humble yet realistic approach to the realities of being part of a family business. His invaluable expertise shines through in thought-provoking exercises that help guide you toward meaningful solutions. Whether navigating succession challenges, resolving conflicts, or building a lasting legacy, his guidance and approach support you through your own personal journey—be it within a family business or beyond. Working with him has been transformative on many levels, personally and professionally.

Alycia Mondavi, Fourth Generation Co-Proprietor, C. Mondavi & Family - United States of America

The study of multi-generational families and families in business has largely hovered around the topics of the management and transition of financial and business wealth. Little time has been afforded to the area of emotional wealth as this is often dynamic and messy. Given this, it is great to see Franco address this topic head on. No amount of structure and governance models will hold a family together if a robust emotional architecture does not exist. Franco outlines some great practical tools and ideas to help families build this vital architecture.

Sach Chandaria, Fifth Generation Family Member, Board Member of Family Business Network (FBN) International–Switzerland

The blend of narrative story telling with actionable frameworks makes the ideas resonate whether you are seeking personal growth, improving family harmony or guiding a family business through succession. If you want to understand how past generations subtly shape present choices, this book offers a thoughtful starting place.

Anton Oliver, Former New Zealand All Blacks Captain and Co-Founder of Athletes Trust - Thailand

Francesco Lombardo, through *What Your Parents Didn't Tell You*, brings a rare blend of honesty, practical wisdom, and deep compassion to the subject of family legacies and emotional inheritance. This book gives readers the tools to identify and break negative patterns. Francesco weaves together personal stories (including his own, where he shows incredible insight, bravery and vulnerability), historical and real life examples. At the end of each chapter he pauses with questions to ponder which invite real self-reflection. He tackles tough topics - shame, addiction, grief, and the 'impostor' within - with clarity and empathy.

Whether you're in a family business, navigating generational change, or looking to understand emotional patterns, this book is invaluable. It's grounded and insightful. Francesco reminds us that emotional wealth is just as critical as financial wealth - and that with courage, structure and authenticity, families can continue a wonderful legacy.

Catherine Sayer, CEO, Family Business Association Australia–Australia

Franco covers what most succession plans, in my experience, overlook; the impact of emotion. Unspoken rules and narratives passed down through generations that can sustain or silently sabotage a legacy.

What Your Parents Didn't Tell You is a must read for generative families and their advisors. By sharing deeply personal experiences, easily digestible synopses of research from diverse fields of study, anecdotal stories and compelling metaphors, Franco provides helpful insights and practical frameworks for families wanting to improve their chances of protecting financial and non-financial capital for generations.

This book is for anyone who wants to understand how inherited emotional patterns influence identity, relationships and decision-making. It interacts with the reader in a very personal way and has much actionable material that is relevant to any family that is hopeful of building a lasting legacy, one defined by connection as much, if not more than, wealth

Iain Blakeley, Founding Chair, New Zealand Family Business Association–New Zealand

Most families believe they are transferring wealth. In reality, they are transferring an emotional operating system.

In *What Your Parents Didn't Tell You*, Francesco Lombardo names the hidden inheritance that shapes identity, relationships, and long-term continuity: the emotional traditions we normalize—and the truths we avoid. This is not a sentimental book about feelings. It is a serious framework for emotional governance, and a timely reminder that no amount of financial sophistication can compensate for an unaddressed emotional legacy.

If you care about the future of a family—read this."

Ryna Mi, Architect of Sovereign Wealthcare and Founding Steward of The Wealth School–Switzerland

Honest, authentic and real insights into family dynamics and how experiences growing up inevitably shape our thoughts and influence behaviours throughout a lifetime. Real insights. Real perspectives. Real questions.

Family business matters but we all need to be honest, courageous and have an appreciation of how the past inevitably influences the future for us all.

Paul Andrews, CEO, Family Business United–United Kingdom

In *What Your Parents Didn't Tell You*, Franco brings together decades of experience, insight, and compassion. He reveals how emotional legacies—those invisible traditions and patterns passed down through generations—shape our lives, our relationships, and our futures. This book is not just a guide for families of means; it is a call to anyone seeking to understand the deeper currents that influence their decisions, their sense of belonging, and their capacity for growth.

This read is essential for anyone who wishes to leave a legacy that is not only prosperous, but also meaningful and lasting.

Hilton Sacks, EVP, Head of International Development at Cidel Private Bank–Canada

His latest book, *What Your Parents Didn't Tell You–How Hidden Family Truths Shape Your Life & Future*, is a fascinating tale as to "What is Emotional Legacy". This is a book every family should sit down in a quiet corner and enjoy reading - it is a book that captures every element of one's life and answers so many questions.

I am proud to have known Franco – I am proud that I have been able to introduce him to so many families and I am proud that he has been able to address, help and mend the dysfunctional nature so many families have been experiencing and where they are now enjoying a new meaningful and loving new beginning.

Iain Mason, Executive Chairman, FullBridge Capital – Australia

This book is a must read if you, as a parent, are committed to creating a vision for your family and wealth, as they are inseparable, and each must be designed to support, protect and strengthen the other. In *What Your Parents Didn't Tell You*, Franco gives you the secret to achieving what you might have thought was impossible.

Thane Stenner, Founder, Stenner Wealth Partners of CG Wealth Management – Canada

In family businesses, unlike what too many people think, the greatest risks are rarely on the balance sheet! They live in unspoken assumptions, inherited patterns, and the conversations families tend to avoid. *What Your Parents Didn't Tell You* is a great and inspiring segway that offers a clear framework for building emotional governance: the ability to "feel together", communicate honestly and move forward with TRUST. It's deeply aligned with the work we have been doing at Trusted Family with Franco in helping families create clarity, cohesion, and continuity.

Arnaud de Coninck, CRO, Trusted Family & G6 Solvay Group – Belgium

Finally, a detailed road-map for families to achieve emotional preparedness with their next-gen and navigate the complexities around succession and legacy-building. Franco has juxtaposed his decades of experience advising families with excellent historical narratives to guide any family through overcoming past emotional fractures towards "leaving their jersey in a better place". An essential read for families and their advisors in a make-or-break space for family succession, which is often left unaddressed.

Tandip Singh Wasan, CEO, Altrui Investment Management (SFO) – Singapore

It doesn't matter if you see yourself as an individual, or from the family principal / family member point of view: This is great insight, bursting with deep experience and helpful advice. Highly recommended!

Tobias Prestel, Founding Partner, Prestel and Partner (Family Office Forum Events Worldwide) – Dubai

What Your Parents Didn't Tell You names something most of us feel but rarely have language for: the invisible emotional patterns that shape our families, our leadership, and our lives.

Having spent decades working with families, founders, and next-generation leaders, I've seen firsthand how unspoken emotional legacies—more than strategy, governance, or wealth—determine whether families thrive or fracture over time. This book brings clarity to that reality with rare depth, courage, and humanity.

Francesco Lombardo doesn't approach family dynamics from a place of blame, but from responsibility. He shows that emotional wealth is not soft or abstract—it is foundational. When ignored, it quietly undermines everything we try to build. When understood and intentionally stewarded, it becomes one of the greatest gifts we can pass on.

This is an important book for anyone thinking about legacy—not just what they leave behind, but what they leave *within* the people they love.

Stephen Hecht, Co-Founder & Chief Executive Peacemaker, Million Peacemakers

What Your Parents Didn't Tell You

What Your Parents Didn't Tell You

ISBN (paperback): 978-1-963271-65-2
ISBN (ebook): 978-1-963271-64-5

ARMINLEAR

Armin Lear Press, Inc.
215 W Riverside Drive, #4362
Estes Park, CO 80517

What Your Parents Didn't Tell You

How Hidden Family Truths Shape Your Life and Future

Francesco Lombardo

I dedicate this book to my children. As they have become adults, they've been among my greatest teachers and have inspired me to become the best possible version of myself.

They have reminded me what matters most and contributed to the creation of the emotional legacy I want to leave behind, with them and my future generations.

I dedicate this book to you, the reader, for being curious, brave, wanting more than a financial legacy. For contributing to supporting my life's purpose of wanting to create a safer world for all of us.

You have the ability to be an instrument for transformation; this book is your guide.

And finally, I dedicate this book to my clients, who have entrusted me with their families and their emotional legacies. For coming along for the journey to the summit, for being committed to wanting different emotional safety in the family. You are the reason I do this work. Thank you for allowing me to follow my dream of creating a safer world.

Contents

Foreword

It's rare to find a book that doesn't simply share insights but reveals truths, truths that make you pause, breathe deeply, and re-evaluate the very foundations upon which your identity rests. *What Your Parents Didn't Tell You* is that kind of book.

Franco Lombardo has spent decades working with some of the world's wealthiest families, names you may never hear in the headlines, yet whose influence quietly shapes industries, economies, and communities. But this book isn't about them. It's about us. It's about you. It's about the emotional legacies we all carry, often unknowingly, and the hidden scripts that govern how we show up in relationships, in business, in parenting, and in life.

I first met Franco years ago, not in a formal boardroom or high-stakes investment meeting, but on a muddy trail in the Amazon jungle. We were part of an immersive leadership experience, one that brought together changemakers and visionaries to strip back the layers of privilege and power and return to something simpler: purpose. Even in those early conversations, I could see that Franco wasn't interested in the masks people wear. He was drawn to the why behind the what, to the wounds behind the wealth, to the unsaid stories behind the family photos. In the years since, I've watched him walk beside families through some of their most vulnerable moments, not with judgment or ego, but with humility, courage, and compassion.

This book is a culmination of that journey.

In *What Your Parents Didn't Tell You*, Franco pulls back the curtain on a phenomenon that touches nearly every family of means: the silent inheritance. It's not the legal trusts or real estate portfolios. It's the unconscious beliefs, the unprocessed traumas, the emotional behaviors passed down like heirlooms from one generation to the next. These legacies don't show up on a balance sheet, but they determine how a family navigates success, conflict, intimacy, and identity.

You won't find generic advice or recycled tropes in these pages. What you'll find instead is an invitation to get curious. To ask yourself questions that might feel uncomfortable, even confronting:

What role did I unconsciously inherit in my family, and is it serving me now?

When I say, "I want my children to be happy," do I actually know what that looks like, or am I just projecting my unresolved needs onto them?

Am I building wealth… or just perpetuating pain in more sophisticated packaging?

Franco's insights are not merely academic. They are lived, hard-earned, and at times deeply personal. He shares openly from his own story, including the parts many of us might shy away from, his own wounds, his growth, and the hard lessons that shaped his approach. That honesty is not a performance. It's the very foundation of the trust he has built with families who let him into their most sacred spaces: the spaces where money meets meaning.

One of the most powerful concepts explored in this book is what Franco calls the *Money Myth*—the deeply ingrained, often subconscious beliefs we hold about money. These mottos are formed early, and they influence everything: how we invest, how we give, how we measure worth, and how we define enough. For many of Franco's clients, identifying their Money Myth is like being handed a mirror for the first time in their adult lives. It allows them to see not just what they do, but *why* they do it.

But what I admire most about this book isn't its framework. It's its heart.

Franco never loses sight of the humanity within the families he serves. Behind every legacy is a longing—to be seen, to be safe, to be loved. Behind every family system is a child, no matter their age, trying to reconcile who they were taught to be with who they truly are. This book doesn't claim to have all the answers. Instead, it gives you permission, and the tools, to start asking better questions.

There's a myth that wealthy families don't suffer. That access, education, and influence insulate them from the deeper wounds of abandonment, addiction, perfectionism, or fear of not being enough. However, as Franco makes clear in these pages, money is not a balm. In many cases, it's an accelerant. It magnifies the cracks in relationships and exposes the fault lines in values. If left unchecked, it can pass those fractures forward to the next generation with even greater velocity.

But here's the hope: awareness is the first step to change.

This book is not a condemnation. It's a map. A guide for those who are ready to move from unconscious inheritance to intentional legacy. It's for those who understand that true wealth has less to do with net worth and more to do with self-worth. It's for those brave enough to explore their story, not to assign blame, but to rewrite the ending.

I've worked with families across the globe, some of great means, some with almost nothing, and what I've learned is this: all families want the same thing. They want to love and be loved. They want to leave something better behind. They want to belong. Wanting isn't enough. You have to do the work. *What Your Parents Didn't Tell You* is a powerful catalyst for that work.

Franco's wisdom is hard-won. It's forged in years of walking beside families through their defining moments: transitions, deaths, divorces, reconciliations, and rebirths. His courage lies not in telling people what they want to hear, but what they need to hear. This book is no exception.

If you're reading this foreword, it's because something in you is ready. Ready to face your story. Ready to lead differently. Ready to parent with greater presence. Ready to heal what was hidden. Ready to become the author of your own legacy, rather than just the inheritor of someone else's.

So read with an open heart. Reflect honestly. Above all, be gentle with yourself. Healing takes time. Integration takes courage. The journey is worth it.

In the end, the greatest inheritance we can give, or receive, is the truth.

Craig Kielberger Co-Founder Legacy +
New York Times Best Selling Author of
What is My Legacy? Realizing a New Dream of
Connection, Love and Fulfillment
With Mr. and Mrs. King

INTRODUCTION

What is An Emotional Legacy?

An emotional legacy underlies why you behave and react the way you do, why you see the world the way you do.

Emotional legacy is the lasting imprint a person leaves on others because of emotional memories they created. It is passed down in a family or group that may determine how that family operates and moves through the world for hundreds of years. These emotional traditions are like everything you face day-to-day as you move through a complex world.

In my work with families inextricably tied to a business they share, several generations may have, or had, presided over regional and international activities and perhaps thousands of people. They unify their vision under an identity, a brand, a mission statement, and a culture. They want to sustain that vision by doing everything they can to ensure that others—especially their own families—feel their presence and achievements long after they're gone.

Why does anyone bring a visionary offering to the world? Some entrepreneurs see an opportunity in the market and decide to seize it by starting a business. Other visionaries see a deficiency in the community around them and decide to create a cultural movement to resolve it. An underlying driver of both is their belief that what they are doing is somehow an improvement on what previously existed in that space. No matter how hard they work, no matter how many hours they devote to the venture, they believe that what they are doing matters. Whether they realize or not, they are developing habits and patterns of behavior that will leave a lasting psychological and relational imprint on the people closest to them.

Let me take you into a world I know well—and what I've learned through the decades is that this world teaches all of us a lot about how an emotional legacy takes shape.

In the business world, 70 percent of businesses fail during leadership transition from the first generation to the second—from parent to child. Out of the 30 percent that do make it, only 28 percent survive the next transition, from the second generation to the third. And of those 28 percent, only 12 percent survive the transition from the third generation to the fourth. Financial security does not guarantee the *emotional* security of a family. And that's just in family businesses. There are millions of families in the world and not all of them have business. Yet, the underlying negative emotional traditions and the behavioral patterns they cause can have the same effect on anyone. How can this happen?

Every family has a set of rules, narratives, biases and preferences that govern how emotions are managed in the family system. These rules and narratives become normalized into a set of beliefs about the world. In order to maintain a family, we create traditions. Some of them can be destructive. We call this ecology of beliefs a family's *emotional tradition*. We have all heard, or maybe have even said ourselves, the litany of self-limiting beliefs around how we live our emotional lives. We tell ourselves stories like “I’m not good enough;” or “I’m too impulsive” about our emotions and these stories can become the set of rules that define how we walk through the world.

Emotional traditions are a set of behaviors and values that are passed down from parent to offspring. As a family grows and new generations are added to the family, these emotional traditions are passed down. Sometimes, they are modified and overwritten with new emotional traditions that are themselves passed down. This conveyor belt of emotional traditions that are passed down the generations color and flavor a family’s *emotional legacy.*

Consider a glass of orange juice. The juice of an orange is only as good as the soil in which it’s grown. To know how good or bad an orange will taste, you have to know where the orange tree was planted and what kind of juice it created before. Then you need to capture that information and determine the steps necessary to create the kind of juice you want. Similarly, a young boy or girl has an emotional legacy instilled in them by their parents.

I have worked with some of the world’s most prominent and successful families, helping them transform their succession plans into an opportunity to repair deeply ingrained generational wounds. Doing this work, I have witnessed emotional traditions within families erupting to the surface from all angles and the similarities are striking. I have identified **ten emotional patterns carried over lifetimes** that show up in families with negative emotional traditions:

1. **Not feeling safe to express themselves:** A child throws a temper tantrum, and the parent says, “I don’t like you right

now," leading the child to feel they can never express their emotions with their family. Even as an adult, expressing emotions is not safe.

2. **The legacy is more important than family:** A parent spends a lot of time, focus and energy at work, or focused on a passion like re-building classic cars. The legacy becomes an extra sibling—and maybe the child feels like they matter less than the parent's favorite "child."

3. **Emotional abandonment:** A parent isn't around, so the kids aren't learning how to handle their emotions well. There is nobody—or no system in place—to help teach them that emotions are important and how to handle them. Parents may even handle conflict by screaming at each other. They don't have a proper conversation. The child thinks, "that's how to act and get my needs met."

4. **Lack of emotional connection/awareness:** The parent hasn't done work to develop emotional awareness, modeling zero emotional awareness for the child. The child grows up and is about to face adversity with no real childhood experience of adversity. They are unprepared.

5. **It's not okay to share**: When a family member tries to share their feelings, they are ridiculed. They decide there's no point in sharing their emotions. This is something that carries over into adulthood and affects every aspect of one's life.

6. **Shame:** It is incredibly common for members of the next generation to feel shame or guilt about being born into the family, but they never bring it up. Others may look at them with envy, unfairly calling them "entitled brat," or other names which become internalized. They feel helpless to do anything about it.

7. **Obsession with status:** Some family members like to see their name on mastheads, even if they aren't contributing much. They have a desire to be seen and heard by everyone, except the people inside their home. Some families are very generous externally (through their philanthropic work) but aren't emotionally generous with each other at home.

8. **Superficial conversations:** Family members don't know how to have intimate conversations, so they don't. They have conversations that are meaningless. They create filler-talk for silence. Conversations like this don't drive the family forward. There is no meaning behind them and no deeper connections are created.

9. **Using money as control:** Parents may try to control their children with it. For better or for worse, they use money like a doggy treat—you only get it if you do what I want. A parent also could have been showering their children with money and gifts for so long to buy their love while they emotionally abandon them. To the child, money then becomes a conundrum.

10. **Difficulty with saying "No":** Sometimes children do not want to say "no" to their parent when asked if they want to steward the family legacy—whether in the form of a business or family role. They don't want to upset their parent, especially after seeing how hard that parent worked to build a legacy that could be transferred to another generation. However, parents can also have a tough time saying "no" when their child claims they're ready to take on a new role with more responsibility within the family, but the parent doesn't feel the same.

These are only some of the most universal emotional patterns and emotional traditions and there are many more. Here's the good news: We are not stuck with these patterns, or the family emotional traditions that have been handed down through the generations.

We can break those patterns—we *have* to break those patterns, or the patterns will break *us*.

Much of this book—how to take over, let go and move on. With the poor success rate of transitioning businesses or assets from one generation to the next, with every one of these financial transitions that fails, there is likely a family being broken up and relationships breaking down. The result of this is the founder's efforts, dedication and commitment to creating the vision, the business or the wealth in the first place isn't intact down the generations.

The thing is, many of these same patterns and mechanics apply just as easily to families without a family business. This is because we are overlooking one of the most important dynamics of human life, one that influences many of our decisions, all of our relationships and might determine our life outcomes: Our feelings. As founders, entrepreneurs, creators, and visionaries of any kind, we understand the necessity of designing our futures but in all our calculations, are we factoring in the gravity of emotions?

An emotional legacy can be a catalyst for excellence, driving a new generation inheriting that legacy to great success. It can also be a barrier or dampening force that prevents the inheriting generation of a business from feeling ready for the opportunity and danger of inheriting the family legacy. It can cause a conflict between those who inherit—who deserves what share of the legacy? It might even cause some to reject their inheritance, leaving the family business to be transferred outside of the family, or liquidated by its shareholders. So, how do we create a formula for succession that won't tear your family apart?

This book reveals one of the greatest secrets in all human history:

Structure can be built for our emotional lives, just as structures can be built for an organization. When we set a course for a positive, emotional future—establishing a new and constructive emotional legacy for our children and future generations—we create **emotional wealth**. This incredible and innovative form of wealth can be passed down to descendants just like money. It is a timeless gift helping to secure both the emotional certainty, relational peace and quite possibly, even the financial security we want for ourselves and our families.

CHAPTER 1

What is Emotional Wealth?

A rich person is someone who has assets. In the context of our look at family and connections, a wealthy person has a relationship with their feelings.

At the end of life most people don't say, "I wish I'd bought that $800 raincoat." We can enjoy things while we're alive, but at the end of our lives, most of our thoughts are more likely to go to our loved ones; our friends, our families, and the lives we've touched. We will judge ourselves by the feelings we hold about the impact we've had on our relationships and maybe even the world. Whatever you own, whatever you build or achieve in life, the value you place on your inner life—your feelings—exceeds the value of your possessions or privileges.

The Danger of Money

Drew Barrymore's journey to happiness illuminates the point. She was born in 1975 in Culver City, California to an esteemed American family with three generations of actors. Her father, actor John Drew

Barrymore, had left her mother, aspiring actress Jaid Barrymore, only months before Drew was born.

Growing up between West Hollywood and the Sherman Oaks neighborhood of Los Angeles, Drew was exposed to the fast-paced and frenetic world of acting practically from infancy, starring in a dog food commercial at eleven months old. The young Drew was thrust into a life of performance and scrutiny while most children were learning the very basics of how the world worked.

It was her meeting Steven Spielberg shortly after that would form one of the most impactful relationships of the little girl's life. While casting his landmark film *E.T. The Extra-Terrestrial* Spielberg encountered the precocious Drew who regaled him with elaborate stories of her time leading a Punk band—still in vogue in the early 1980s. Spielberg felt her imagination was so electric that he cast her as Gertie—the mischievous little sister in the film. Spielberg would become Drew's godfather and a steady and protective father-figure in her life. "Nobody treated me like a kid there," Drew would later say about the cast of *E.T.* Her life as an accessory to her aspiring actress mother, performing for her approval, had created a conflict in her. She had been robbed of her childhood and yet wanted to be recognized as something more than a child.

E.T. was one of the highest grossing films of the decade, catapulting Drew into fame and success. Seemingly overnight, Drew Barrymore became one of the most recognized child actors of the era. No child is ready for the power and demands of stardom. Popular recognition, especially in the entertainment industry, can arrive suddenly, and at any time. For some, it comes after decades of hard work and the seasoning of adulthood. For others it can arrive before a person grows up enough to understand who they are, what their values are, and what they want out of life. For a young girl, like Drew, primed and conditioned to *perform* as perhaps the only valid way to matter, this sudden achievement was unexpected.

Time after time, we've seen many who experience great success or sudden riches suffer with addiction and self-destructive behaviors. How can this happen when we think that money, status and success will be the salve for a lifetime of struggle and failure? Even as a teenage girl, she was a fixture at feverish parties at Studio 54 in Manhattan—a music venue and nightclub throughout the 1970s and 1980s famous for extravagant parties, disco hedonism and drug use. By age thirteen, Drew's mother had checked her into rehab. Shortly after, Drew tried to commit suicide. An emotional tradition of performance and public recognition had driven a young girl, denied a typical childhood with an intact and emotionally connected family, and the ability to grow up in private out of the limelight, into the extreme regulation of addiction and the flight-response of attempting suicide.

We all have emotional triggers that cause us to react. These are our automatic behavioral responses, and they form when we are young. As Drew grew up, she got clean and worked on understanding the emotional tradition she grew up in. She would use her troubled youth—the only world she knew—as the underpinning of the roles she would play throughout the 1980s and 1990s, her roles in *Irreconcilable Differences* and *Far From Home* which made her a cultural icon and further elevated her success.

It was her being exposed to a set of emotional traditions beyond the ones she had grown up with that would begin to shift Drew out of her tumultuous adolescence and into adult distinction. In 1995, Drew would pose nude for *Playboy*. In response, her godfather,

Steven Spielberg, sent her a beautiful handmade quilt for her twentieth birthday, complete with an attached note which read, "Cover Up." It would spur Drew to claim an identity for herself on healthier terms. The guidance of others with a different emotional tradition, one of dignity, class and high-personal standards, would help influence Drew to set a new tone in her life.

When we are unprepared for something, even success, it can be dangerous because we don't yet understand the gravity and responsibility that goes along with any kind of achievement. When we don't have the coordinates to navigate the storm of attention, opportunities and demands that success creates, we could implode, or perhaps we might tear ourselves apart trying to meet conflicting demands. The confusion and overload can become overwhelming and create a desire inside of us to regulate ourselves with illicit substances, alcohol, sex, or other addictions.

Money can be dangerous because it can insulate us from awareness of our inner emotional landscape. When we suddenly or finally attain great financial wealth, it can distract us from looking inward and understanding the emotional traditions that we grew up with and how those emotional traditions inform the way we move through the world; they influence our relationships, our choices and what we tell ourselves about *ourselves*.

Feelings: Liabilities or Assets?

Some people see feelings as liabilities—inconvenient, childish indulgences that disrupt productivity and cause problems. They override them.

We may not be fully aware that we want to *feel* like we're in control—instead of being driven by something inside of us that just happens, without our direct command. Maybe we don't take the time to know and understand our feelings, the mechanics of emotions, or why we have them. If we engage in a process to understand them fully, we might see they are among our greatest assets—for ourselves and for others.

Most leaders in companies understand the concept of human capital—an array of professional skills and expertise that can be leveraged for the success of the business. But when we think about human capital, we tend to only include hard skills. Few consider the emotional dimensions of human capital—the soft skill of understanding one's feelings. What if, just as we would have a financial balance sheet to manage our monetary accounts, we include a *Human Capital Balance Sheet* and a *Social Capital Balance Sheet*?

- A **Human Capital Balance Sheet** could show us who we are individually—our skills, knowledge, strengths, even weaknesses, and also our emotional and perceptual awareness, and our self-awareness; it's a complete picture of the whole individual, inside and out.

- B **Social Capital Balance Sheet** could show us who we are collectively—our family, groups, the institutions we have relationships with and the dynamics of those relationships.

Gathering that kind of data would be a huge undertaking, but we're already equipped with the skills to do it. It starts with the right kind of communication and the right kind of listening and human beings have been doing this for hundreds of thousands of years. First, we must start with ourselves. During this process any beliefs and narratives we uncover are potentially our liabilities. Our goal is to transform them into assets.

What Humans Need

Born in 1908 to Russian-Jewish immigrant parents, Abraham Maslow grew up in poverty to eventually become a celebrated American psychologist and philosopher. Throughout his career he became a prominent voice towards humanizing psychology by focusing on the whole person rather than reducing a person to a set of clinical symptoms. In 1943, Maslow identified a set of basic human needs that were essential motivation for an individual human being to thrive. He built these overlapping needs into a framework that academics and others later modeled into a pyramid, somewhat erroneously depicting a hierarchy:

Physiological Needs: These are biological necessities for survival—our most primal drives.

Air, food, water
Shelter, sleep
Clothing, warmth
Reproduction (sex)

Safety Needs: Once our physical needs are met, humans then seek safety, security, predictability, and stability.

Personal security (shelter, freedom from violence, emotional security)
Health and well-being
Financial security (employment, resources)
Safety nets against accidents/illness

Love and Belonging Needs: Humans are inherently social beings. Loneliness and social isolation can severely impact well-being and survival.

Family connections

Friendships

Intimacy and romantic relationships

Social groups, community, and inclusion

Esteem Needs: There are two types: the need for respect from others (recognition) and the need for self-respect (confidence, mastery).

Self-respect, self-esteem and confidence

Recognition, achievement

Status and reputation

Feeling valued and respected by others

Self-Actualization: This is about realizing your full potential and it's unique to each person.

Personal growth and peak experiences

Creativity, problem-solving

Pursuing meaning, morality, truth

Becoming "the most that one can be"

What Maslow highlighted is that, even if the fundamental biological drivers of human behaviors are identical, no two people are the same. We all have our own quirks. Our own desires. Our preferred way of doing things, of saying things, and of expressing ourselves. Individuality is something to be celebrated, and we see this today more than ever. Many psychologists, philosophers, gurus and thought leaders around the world have adapted Maslow's hierarchy of needs to suit the challenges of the time.

Motivational speaker Anthony Robbins has reworked Maslow's concept into his idea of **Six Basic Human needs:** certainty, uncertainty/variety, significance, love/connection, growth, and contribution. These needs get the spotlight in chapter 4. For now, the key takeaway is that conflicts between biological drivers (such as safety) and emotional needs (such as unbridled passion) are integral to shaping what we call society.

How Feelings Build Societies

Feelings influence most decisions. According to the American Psychological Association's Dictionary of Psychology, a feeling is "a self-contained phenomenal experience… subjective, evaluative, and independent of the sensations, thoughts, or images evoking them." When we describe our feelings, we're describing our subjective experience of physiological changes in our bodies that connect to either comfort, or discomfort. These changes can be caused by direct experiences, physical sensations, our thoughts, our behaviors and the behaviors of others.

However, there's a twist in our understanding of human feelings and how it isn't just feelings alone that can drive us to act in the service of a set of values or actions. Lucius Annaeus Seneca—a Roman statesman who lived during the first century CE said, "We suffer more in imagination than in reality." What Seneca was describing is that, when human beings experience a feeling, we tell ourselves a *story* about that feeling. The same story repeated over time becomes a *pattern*. That pattern carried over a lifetime becomes an *emotional tradition*.

Over time, emotional traditions can become so deeply ingrained that they can act almost like an instinct. Those instinctive reactions evolved to help us survive and navigate our environment—especially our social environment. Imagine that you are a human being living 10,000 years ago in a tribe of hunter-gatherers. Food is scarce, predators are abundant, rival tribes live just over the next hill. Your ability to understand the environment, survive natural disasters, or adapt to changing conditions is limited.

Living in a small band of 100-200 people, you might only know those few hundred people your entire life. If you found yourself shunned, or cast out of the tribe, you became immediately vulnerable—facing the dangers of the environment alone. With so many varied and imminent dangers, our human ancestors needed a system of close social bonds to survive.

To create stable societies, humans used mythology, stories and rituals that engaged feelings and emotions and directed them to a specific set of values that created those social bonds. The same emotional ties to competence, authority and strength that kept a tribal chieftain in power on the Eurasian steppes in 4,000 BCE. keeps the president of a business in the boardroom. The same ties and traditions that enabled hunters to hunt in coordinated bands and gatherers to communicate vital information to each other enable modern teams to collaborate and produce.

When organizations and individuals set out to build something—a business, a home, a relationship—we are optimizing for a set of conditions that will meet a specific need. We attach feelings to whatever we are optimizing for. While our human instinctive emotional responses have not evolved much beyond where they were 10,000 years ago in our ancestral past, the stories we tell ourselves about those emotions have. Sometimes, because of the stories we tell ourselves about our own feelings, those instinctive emotional responses can be out of step with our environment, causing us discomfort in many forms both emotional and psychological. When we notice a maladaptive reactive pattern playing out in some area of our life, the first thing we need to examine is **what is that instinctive pattern telling us** and **what is that pattern optimizing for?**

What Are You Optimizing For?

In a move considered by many to be controversial and high risk, Elon Musk purchased Twitter in 2022 for $44 billion. Musk was so certain about his decision to purchase the platform that pledged a great deal of his Tesla stock as collateral and sold shares, committing another $21 billion of his own assets to effect the acquisition.

Musk's purchase of Twitter was fiercely debated between partisan political factions. Camp A argued that Twitter had become ideologically biased, favoring the opinions and media of culturally sanctioned and approved left-wing activists while censoring and suppressing all other points of view. Camp B argued that Musk's calls for free speech and his public assurances that purchasing Twitter was an attempt to restore free speech to American discourse was nothing more than a smokescreen to cover-up a politicized agenda: the platforming of Donald Trump-aligned narratives to sway public opinion. Other social media platforms, such as Facebook (Meta) and YouTube, had previously been accused of similar biased platforming in favor of President Joe Biden's 2020 election campaign.

Both ideological camps—each viewing the other with suspicion—might have been optimizing for the same thing: Preeminence in the media landscape and the assurance that their emotional tradition, and eventually emotional legacy, will have a dominant foothold in the *zeitgeist*.

Throughout 2023, Musk's acquisition of Twitter dominated the media landscape. He immediately discharged CEO Parag Arawal and CFO Ned Segal leading to Twitter's stock being delisted from the New York Stock Exchange. His firing of over half of Twitter's 7500 staff was heavily scrutinized in the press, leading to speculation that the company would quickly collapse and even causing wrongful-termination lawsuits. Musk issued decrees that any employees remaining with the transforming company should anticipate "long, intense hours of work." In November of 2022 *The Verge* had reported that key engineering teams working at the nerve-center of the company "completely or near-total[ly] resigned." To the outside world, the upheaval in Musk's Twitter resembled the kinetic *coup d'etats* of any dictatorship.

Why would a leader make such sweeping and drastic structural changes to a company? What was Elon Musk optimizing for? Increasing his profits by acquiring one of the largest and most influential social media platforms in history—used by journalists, celebrities and world leaders? Were the mass-layoffs about efficiency, or a dictator-like consolidation of power and influence—the elimination of potential sources of trouble to the new power structure? By the 2024 U.S. Presidential Election, it became clear that Musk might have been optimizing for something else: The potential to have a powerful voice of influence in a new presidential administration and, for better or for worse, the culture and emotional traditions it would create.

Leading up to his 2022 acquisition of Twitter, Musk had built infamy as a cultural pundit, often weighing-in with controversial takes in a frenetic online discourse. Our inner emotional landscape directly influences what we optimize for. Those influences can be directed and conscious or indirect and unconscious. When we understand the stories we carry inside of us about our own experiences, we can optimize for conditions and outcomes with greater intentionality.

Net-worth vs. Net-assets in Terms of Emotional Wealth

So far, we have talked about how emotional traditions form in individuals and within societies. Human societies are made up of families and families create their own emotional traditions. Every human being is someone's son, or daughter, maybe a brother, or sister, a father or mother. In today's highly competitive and fast-paced world of influencers and personalities, we tend to define a person's net-worth by their material success but what if there's another metric for determining the wealth and efficacy of individuals and groups?

In business we define *wealth* as a great quantity of money , possessions, assets, and so on. These are tangible things, however, intangibles such as feelings impact the tangible world, specifically, the human body. Science has explored the relationship between our feelings and the body. In his 2014 book *The Body Keeps the Score: Brain, Mind, and Body in the Healing of Trauma*, psychologist and researcher, Bessel A. van der Kolk writes, "the imprint left by that experience on mind, brain, and body. This imprint has ongoing consequences for how the human organism manages to survive in the present." So if we understand that our experiences cause us to have feelings, and those feelings leave a physical imprint on the body, why would we not consider our feelings an asset?

Conceptual artist, author and culturist Jamie Mustard (*The Iconist*) draws a clear distinction between the concept of net-worth and net-assets. "What our society currently defines as a person's net-worth," Mustard argues, "is really their net-assets. The net-worth of any human being could only be defined as your meaning and your human relationships." Without understanding this distinction, chaos can ensue in your life.

This means that when you build emotional wealth and infuse it with a sense of direction within your family, you can leave it for your descendants to inherit just as you would financial wealth. For this to be possible, emotional wealth must become your priority. The quality of your relationships, the story you tell about the meaning you attach to what you build, and the stories you tell yourself about your own feelings—if done in full awareness—can ensure happiness and satisfaction for those who come after you.

Optimizing Towards a Positive Emotional Tradition

Here is where we bring together the concepts of emotional tradition, and the amplification of emotional traditions by money and success. In 2022 YouTube had become one of the most influential and lucrative social platforms on Earth. With ad revenue of $29 billion, the platform had exploded from its humble beginnings in 2009 to a cultural powerhouse with over 2.5 billion active users. Merely one year out of a global pandemic, and with economic turmoil occurring worldwide, for many YouTube was becoming not just a lifestyle, but a full-time job.

One YouTuber creating content under the moniker Mr. Beast—American online personality and businessman, James Stephen

Donaldson, known for his ostentatious dares and public contests—posted a Twitter poll: "If someone offered you $10,000 but if you take it a random person on earth dies, would you take the $10,000?" A torrent of responses ensued, and the now infamous poll received 1,894,281 votes. 46 percent of the voters said, "Yes."

Among those who responded, "Yes," how many of them were serious? How many of them considered that the random person dropping dead somewhere on Earth might be their child, their mother, Meryl Streep, a small boy waiting for a kidney transplant, a girl fleeing an oppressive regime in Sudan, or a soldier on a battlefield? Did an impulsive or performative "Yes" show that they think human connection with a "random person" is worthless, regardless of who that person is? A person who answers "Yes" to the question could lack empathy, appreciation for unconditional love, and other qualities that equip someone to have healthy relationships; they could come from an emotional tradition where those things *weren't* present or valued and be reacting out of spite.

The bright side of the amplification effect is that, if you have built a sound emotional structure as the foundation for your emotional wealth, you can be among the 54 percent who said, "No." Your emotional wealth will amplify your drive toward secure connections and those who inherit your emotional tradition can bring it forward and even improve it for future generations. Understanding that emotional wealth is a tangible asset in our lives is just the beginning. We also have to understand that, if you have a weak or unrealized emotional structure, those who come after you—whether living in a multi-million-dollar mansion or a slum—will be sure to be impoverished financially and on a human level.

Questions to ponder:

1. How can money—whether you have it or not—be dangerous in your life?

2. What are you optimizing for—in your day-to-day work, values and relationships?

3. What are your net-assets in terms of emotional wealth?

4. How have any big successes you've had in your life impacted your values, choices, and relationships?

CHAPTER 2

How Do Emotions Help You Predict the Future?

Feelings and the stories we attach to those feelings are the construction material of the emotional lives that we live and that our children will live, and their children will live, and so on. Emotions have a tangible value. A person can create emotional wealth by mapping out their emotional landscape and building a structure for it.

One of the oldest and most celebrated expressions of emotion is art. Mythology, drama, and literature—some of the oldest forms of storytelling, use our individual and collective emotional commonality to convey ideas of meaning and the lives we aspire to.

Pip and Paul

Writing in the mid-19th century, British author Charles Dickens used his novels to explore the social class system of Victorian England. One of his most iconic rags-to-riches novels, *Great Expectations*, published in 1861, follows the adventures of a seven-year-old orphan boy, Philip "Pip" Pirrip, from his impoverished beginnings in Kent to wealth and success and all of the pitfalls along the way. Packed with adventure and intrigue—escaped convicts, prison hulks, chains, an ageing jilted bride living her old age in a faded wedding dress, a beautiful yet hostile love interest, burning mansions, and the filth, grime, and character of Victorian London—Pip is given the opportunity, by a mysterious and anonymous benefactor, to become educated. He rises into the middle class in London, eventually becoming a gentleman.

In his journey out of poverty, Pip doesn't necessarily grow into a more moral and self-aware human being. He steals tools and food to help an escaped convict who's threatening to kill him and allows the convict to lie to cover for him. He is ambitious and even a touch entitled but, through a string of irresponsible business failures, he buries himself under a crush of debts and becomes a wanted man. Pip overlooks his friendships, and lusts after the beautiful and hostile Estella—the adopted daughter of his mysterious benefactor who he wrongly assumes is the jilted bride, Miss Havisham. He is jealous and paranoid about the desire Estella elicits in other men and ignores her emotional unavailability and coldness. After Estella declares that she would have no moral qualms using her charms to entrap a rich member of their social clique, Pip pines after her. Estella marries the rich man anyway.

Pip eventually attains a middle-class life after working as a clerk for years in disgrace away from England. Coming from an emotional tradition where he has had little more than the rags on his back, he sees himself as someone who the world acts upon, not a driving force in his own right. Even worse, his passivity and the unearned financial backing from his mysterious benefactor, who turns out to be the convict Abel Magwitch, has set him up for failure: Pip never had to work for his money; it was given to him. Worse, the money prevented him from experiencing the character-building that would have come along with building his own wealth and from recognizing the emotional assets around him—his true friendships and surrogate family.

Pip becomes an affluent gentleman and eventually gets to marry a widowed Estella, but only after years of exile and emotional carnage. When Pip reunites with Estella, it is in the burnt-out ruins of Miss Havisham's house—a metaphor for the destruction of Pip's emotional tradition in his life. We can't reach through the pages and ask Pip, "Was this really worth it?" We have to determine for ourselves how Pip might feel. We have to bring our own emotional landscape to the exploration; we project ourselves onto Pip, wanting for him what we might want for ourselves. After years of churning pain and thwarted ambition, both Pip and Estella have learned—a moment before it's too late—that the only thing that matters is connection.

What Pip finds out by the end of *Great Expectations*, another writer's hero discovers during the course of his rags-to-riches ordeal. Writing around the same time as Charles Dickens—the mid-nineteenth century, American author Horatio Alger was also writing rags-to-riches—or more aptly stated, rags-to-respectability — coming-of-age stories about ambitious American boys transcending their humble circumstances. While Dickens captured the imagination, Alger captured nuance and it's the nuance that matters.

In Alger's melodramatic 1865 junior novel, *Paul Prescott's Charge*, we follow a young man named Paul as he battles to square up his recently deceased father's debts. Paul had lived with his father through his traumas and regrets. Young Paul faces severe hardship, betrayal, and exploitation. He resolves to take only honest work, agreeing to an assortment of jobs and having adventures with many corrupt and kind-hearted people he meets along the way.

No matter how hard it gets, Paul always chooses hard work and his own integrity over the deceit and corruption he sees all around him—even when it seems easier or even justifiable.

Alger's tale is part of an emotional tradition that exists and is sustained at a cultural level by a nation: The American Dream—the belief that anyone, regardless of their circumstances, can rise to great success through hard work and moral strength.

Alger's emotional tradition says, "Connection and meaning is the *true* wealth," showing us that Paul's wealth is in the relationships he has with those around him who *connect* with his emotional tradition of integrity, determination and openness. Paul's choice to have good character is him optimizing for the conditions that lead him to a good life. Paul understands that, whether he has money and success or not, his emotional wealth cannot be taken from him. As long as he maintains his emotional wealth, he will always have high net-assets in terms of his relationships.

The Biology of Emotion

As human beings we usually treat our feelings and emotional responses to what we experience in the world as abstracts that are detached from our physical bodies. We might describe our feelings with physical sensations: "A chill ran down my spine when she said that," or "My head got hot and I could just feel my blood boiling when I saw the news." We have an awareness that our feelings register in our bodies, but we don't see how our natural and normal biological processes can cause our feelings.

Let's examine how our biology can not only influence how our feelings show up in our lives but can also determine the emotional foundation we could be passing on *biologically* to our descendants.

The human body is a complex ecosystem of chemicals and electrical signals. According to 2013 chemical engineering graduate research from Amrit Jalan and Professor William Green, of the Massachusetts Institute of Technology, roughly 37 trillion chemical reactions—necessary for sustaining life—occur in the human body every second. Most of those chemical reactions we never have to even think about and yet they drive some of our most important decisions in life; to take a risky jump from the tree at age 13 or climb down safely; where to go to school and what to study; whom to marry; whether or not to have kids, or if we're ready to have kids; to join a gang or to join the army. All of the biological pressures that we feel are made up of billions of chemical reactions happening behind the scenes.

To sustain life, the human body is engaged in a constant balancing act, trying to keep its various and essential systems operating in a state of equilibrium biologists call *homeostasis*. This is the condition where the human body, just like any other organism, operates best. Homeostasis is maintained by a natural resistance to any change in a system once it is operating at its peak efficiency.

Just as we would want to keep an internal combustion engine operating within certain limits by monitoring temperature, lubrication and airflow, our bodies are constantly monitoring and regulating the systems that keep us alive. Biologists call this monitoring mechanism *allostasis*. When there is a change in the system, the balance of chemical reactions is disrupted, and we experience biological signals that something has changed—one of those signals is what we call human emotion, or a feeling.

If these changes are both stressful and chronic, they can cause wear and tear on the body, that is, they engender *allostatic load.*

Carrying a heavy degree of allostatic load for too long can cause a biological injury to the nervous system in a part of the brain called the stellate ganglion—a bundle of nerves in the human neck that governs the fight-or-flight response. When we experience a traumatic event or a stressor, the stellate ganglion signals to the amygdala to release stress hormones into the bloodstream. These stress hormones are what enable the body to react quickly in response to an imminent threat or sense of danger.

So called by the pioneering team of scientists, soldiers and futurists who discovered it, Operator Syndrome was coined after the phenomenon of U.S. Special Forces Operators who experienced a battery of debilitating post-traumatic stress symptoms that plagued them for years after long deployments: anxiety, hypervigilance, sleeplessness, reactivity, a sense of doom, paranoia, suicidal and homicidal ideation. Despite no longer being on long patrols, where snipers, IEDs and gunfights were a constant occurrence, their amygdala was still actively anticipating threats, flooding their bodies with stress hormones.

Operator Syndrome was not only found to be rampant in the military, it was also identified in all walks of life, from the incarcerated to the suburban homemaker. No matter the exact situation or circumstances that cause traumatic stress, whether poverty, war or even a damaging emotional tradition passed down through a family, all cause this exact same biological injury.

In his 2016 book, *It Didn't Start with You: How Inherited Family Trauma Shapes Who We Are and How to End the Cycle*, author and trauma researcher, Mark Wolynn explores the field of epigenetics—the scientific study of how the expression of genes changes in any organism through a plethora of environmental factors. "Children with a parent who was traumatized during the Cambodian genocide," Wolynn writes, "tend to suffer from depression and anxiety. Similarly, children of Australian Vietnam War veterans have higher rates of suicide than the general population."

A human female is born with all the eggs she will ever carry, the cells that will eventually become her children are exposed to whatever external conditions she is experiencing. If she is surviving a war zone or famine, the high allostatic load she is carrying will infuse her system with stress hormones, potentially changing her biology and affecting the biology of the ova inside her. If that woman under trauma becomes pregnant with a daughter, *that* daughter's eggs, while in-utero, can also be affected. This multigenerational inheritance of epigenetic changes triggered by trauma is still being explored by researchers, so there are many unanswered questions.

So, what does this mean? If proven true, it means that if you experience sustained trauma—enough to change your biology, you could pass that biological stress directly to your children and grandchildren genetically (if you are female) or you could cause a high allostatic load in your children that causes them to experience a biological injury (if you're male or female). This raises the stakes. Emotional traditions aren't just abstractions; they have the potential to have a tangible biological impact on our legacy.

Emotional Governance

If the biological systems we have as human beings are identical, whether rich or poor, we can experience the multigenerational effects of emotions fueled by trauma.

Families build narratives around their circumstances. One family might frame their material wealth and success as a birthright, carved from the ground by the grit and determination of an industrious and almost mythological pioneer, overcoming impossible odds to become someone important. Another family might frame their lack of wealth as the inability to escape oppression. The presence or absence of money itself is perhaps not as important as the values and narratives—the emotional traditions around that money.

A rich family might expect great financial achievements from descending generations, creating an emotional tradition of over-achievement and emotional suppression as necessary to live up to the family's financial emotional tradition. A poor family might see financial achievement as an impossible goal. They might undermine or sabotage the efforts of descending generations to break free from the crush of poverty and excel.

Another family struggling financially might see having assets as an attainable goal that requires teamwork and making personal sacrifices that enable descending generations to ascend to financial stability.

In the first two examples, a narrative is hiding the biological injury caused by the emotional tradition of the family. The third family understands that, if we want our emotional legacies to endure, making life easier and happier with the correct values for generations will be determined by feelings. They installed a system of *emotional governance* to optimize for achievement and success. To have emotional governance means to have your feelings and emotions in such tight regulation that they are an asset not a liability— to you, or to the system you are part of.

Every culture is built of individuals and families. We must understand how feelings will determine a legacy and the financial wellbeing—no matter your class and the fulfillment of your family for generations to come. How can we build a system of *emotional governance* that can influence our emotional system to move a family towards improvement?

Questions to ponder:

1. What narratives does your family have around feelings and how has that narrative affected your life?

2. How do your feelings show up in your body?

3. What do you typically tell yourself about your feelings?

CHAPTER 3

How Are You Affected by Emotional Traditions?

Discovering that families experience emotional consistency, good or bad, through family interaction, we understand how our emotional lives are passed down through stories, values and feelings. We know that, left unexamined and without governance, certain emotional torches passed down can lead to degraded and even harmful outcomes.

But how do we create a system that puts this new awareness of the tangible gravity of emotions to work, not only for ourselves but also for our families? So that we can explore this question, let's first look at a story of a reluctant adventurer, a young man who thrust himself into discomfort and danger to complete a demanding personal quest which had once claimed the life of his father. It's a story of ambition, obsession and the hidden costs of mastering the impossible.

The Mountain Ahead

Towering majestically above the picturesque Lauterbrunnen Valley, high in the Bernese Alps of Switzerland, is the Eiger, a gargantuan

3,967-meter (13,015-foot) mountain considered one of the most challenging climbs in the world.

Perhaps the Eiger's most infamous trait is its North face—an awe-inspiring 1,800-metre (5,900-foot) vertical wall of ice-and snow-covered limestone. This unforgiving North face—the biggest in the Alps—is how the colossal mountain won its name; *Der Eiger* means "The Ogre" in German and it is a monstrous name well earned. For hundreds of years alpinists from all over Europe had summited the mountain from the West or the glaciated South face, but very few had dared to attempt a *direttissima*—a complex and highly-technical direct vertical ascent up the Eiger's treacherous North Face.

For generations, the unconquerable Eiger North Face taunted all who drew near, offering only certain death.

In 1935, two Bavarian Climbers, Karl Mehringer and Max Sedlmeyer attempted a direct line up the Eiger North Face. Within days of leaving their basecamp both men disappeared. Sedlmeyer's body was found a year later in 1936.

Mehringer's remains were eventually discovered by another expedition to the Eiger twenty-five years later in 1962. He had frozen to death 667 meters (2,188 feet) below the summit, at a place now called "death bivouac," named after his harrowing and lonely demise as a warning to other climbers.

It was a biting late-winter day in late March 1966. Famed American mountaineer and alpinist John Harlin II gripped the Eiger's North Face. His team, consisting of Scottish mountaineer Dougal Haston, and German Alpinist Siegfried Hupfauer, had begun their ascent. Harlin had spent years studying the infamous Eiger North Face, determined to prove that a bold *diretissima*—a direct route to the summit— was possible and that he had found it.

The weather conditions on the Eiger during March of 1966 had been harsh and unpredictable. Heavy snowfall obscured many of the mountain's challenging features. Temperatures well below freezing, fierce gusts of winds aloft and frequent and sudden avalanches created treacherous conditions on the mountain.

The stakes were in the stratosphere. The team had corporate backing and had conjured up a storm of media attention; Harlin's gaze was fixed on proving a direct route to the Eiger summit existed. His proposed track, which came to be known as the Harlin Route, was intended to be the straightest possible line to the summit. If he were able achieve this, he would cement his legacy in the climbing world and succeed where few before him had dared.

Delays and setbacks due to the Swiss winter weather and frenetic conditions had forced the team to wait to start their ascent. Finally, in early March 1966, conditions on the Eiger eased and the team began their ascent. By March 22, Harlin and his team had reached a section of vertical wall meters above death bivouac. Cold, dark, and exposed to rock and icefall as the sun hit the mountain, the team employed siege tactics, including fixed ropes, to navigate the increasingly challenging terrain. Avalanches of snow, ice and falling rock increased stress on fixed ropes.

Harlin was steadily ascending a fixed rope, attached above him to the rock, just below the so-called White Spider—a notorious obstacle shaped like a huge, radiating fan of ice-filled crags and gullies that resemble the legs of a spider, when his rope—his lifeline—snapped. Harlin fell about 1,000 meters (roughly 4,000 feet) to his death, landing on the glacier at the base of the North face.

That morning, nine-year-old John Harlin III was living with his family in Leysin, a village in the shadow of the Eiger. It was a Tuesday morning, and shortly after waking, young John heard the dull thump of helicopters circling the expanse of rolling valley between Leysin and the Eiger. Immediately, his heart skipped. Every nerve buzzed in John's body as he sensed that something was wrong and when he emerged onto the streets of the Village, he saw the helicopters flying like carrion birds around the Eiger's monstrous North face. John felt a thick unease in the air, a tension that suggested something had gone terribly wrong.

He didn't hear the news from his mother, Mary Harlin, directly. It was in the combination of overheard conversations and the somber expressions of the adults around him, overshadowing the grandeur and fame of the expedition. His father had left him alone to master the Eiger. Now John felt only a crushing weight on his chest. His father was never coming home. "I didn't see him fall. But I've fallen with him thousands of times in my mind," John would write in his 2007 memoir *The Eiger Obsession: Facing the Mountain That Killed My Father*. "For years, that image of him plummeting through the air haunted me—sometimes heroic, sometimes helpless, sometimes just gone. The Eiger took him and left me with questions I had no words for as a boy."

John Harlin II had been a heroic but distant father. He was a magnetic, ambitious mountaineer with chiseled movie star looks. He established the International School of Mountaineering in Leysin, Switzerland, and was part of a generation of climbers who pushed the limits of what was possible in the Swiss Alps. Intensely driven, focused on making his mark in the climbing world—especially through high-risk, high-reward objectives like the *direttissima* on the Eiger North face—John Harlin II was a mountain of a man, larger than life. Yet because of Harlin II's constant training, guiding, and expeditions to reconnoiter the Eiger, the time father and son spent together was limited. After his death, Harlin III was left with fragmentary memories: flashes of adventure and affection, but not the sustained presence of a nurturing parent.

The loss devastated Harlin III's mother who was now suddenly left to raise him alone in Switzerland. Grief, isolation, and financial hardship became her life after her husband's death. The glamor of the climbing life was gone, and in its place was the burden of single motherhood, mourning, and unanswered questions. Harlin II's death during a bold and media-covered climb turned him into a legend. Harlin III grew up in the shadow of a father who was celebrated for his courage but who had, in very real terms, abandoned him—even if unintentionally.

To Harlin III, his father was both a heroic figure and the source of unresolved grief. He idolized his father while also resenting the ambition that had stolen him. The loss created years-long silences between Harlin III and his mother. Living with such intense inner conflict created an emotional void, one that would influence Harlin III's own choices: John Harlin III would become a climber.

As John Harlin III grew older and started a family of his own—eventually having a daughter, Siena—he felt the conflict that had simmered inside him for nearly 40 years. Was he becoming just like his own father, the father who was willing to risk anything in his pursuit of a legacy, the father he had lost? For Harlin III the only way to lay his inner conflict to rest and bury his grief was to confront the very thing that had killed him. John Harlin III would have to face the Eiger.

In July 2005, with Siena supporting him, John Harlin III summited the Eiger, but this ascent was a reckoning not with the Eiger itself but with his father's emotional legacy of risk and daring against impossible odds. High on the North face when he reached the deadly "White Spider" near the place where his father fell, Harlin III felt he had reached a symbolic point of no return. In that moment, 3,300 meters (10,800 feet) up the Eiger's North face, a wave of grief, courage, and connection passed over Harlin III—all at once. He pushed on. Climbing through that zone was a profound, cathartic act—almost like walking through the threshold between myth, life and death.

John would not take the unproven, treacherous Harlin *direttissima* to the summit. Instead, he would take the 1938 Heckmair Route—the classic line up the Eiger's North Face. In this critical decision John's reconciliation with the mountain that killed his father became in reality a symbolic reconciliation with his father's emotional tradition. He chose more stable conditions to attack the Eiger. Because Harlin III's quest was motivated by the desire to transform his grief into a new emotional legacy, he prepared differently. "The Eiger didn't kill me," Harlin III would write in his 2007 memoir, *The Eiger Obsession: Facing the Mountain That Killed My Father*, "It gave me my father, in a way I'd never known him before. It gave me a story I could live with—and finally, let go of." Harlin III's climb helped redefine the narrative of the Eiger in his family—not just a place of death, but one of reconciliation.

John Harlin III's passion to summit could have easily been a negative obsession—being so proximate to his father's death was an emotion that kicked off two decades of anxiety and fixation. But he took a haunting experience and formed a positive new association with the Eiger.

Our brain stores emotionally charged memories and they can remain a part of us and can drive our behavior. The emotional response can be born out of any circumstance—seeing a parent go through the humiliation of asking for help at the food bank or watching a drunk parent trip and fall down the stairs. Those stairs could be at a homeless shelter or at the Met Gala; for the child, the emotional imprint and its effects can be exactly the same.

John Harlin III was a man possessed by finishing the impossible quest his father had started. His story is not about mountaineering—it's a mythic narrative of a man reconciling a damaged emotional tradition through symbolic action. His decision to meet head-on the site of his deepest wound, surviving it on his own terms, enabled John to perform both a ritual of release and a rebirth into autonomy. He became the father he needed—not only for himself but for his daughter.

The Ascent–A Model for Emotional Governance

Preparing to climb a mountain requires more than mere physical conditioning. Intrepid mountaineers like the Harlins understood that summiting an unforgiving and unpredictable mountain also required mental conditioning, an ability to read the terrain, tune-into the conditions of the weather, and most crucially, planning and preparation. In his quest to conquer the Eiger, John Harlin II had spent years in the Swiss Alps photographing and studying its deadly North Face. He documented the mountain's fickle weather patterns and most importantly, he tapped the human assets around him—other mountaineers—for useful information about the Eiger's nuances.

Experienced mountain climbers have planned and prepared for years for their ascent only to be denied their summit victory by the weather. In those critical moments what enables a climber to summit, or turn back to save their life, is the ability to analyze the conditions and *act*.

Sometimes, life can feel just like this. Life is full of emotional storms that can cause us to fight, freeze, or flee. Everything starts with a decision, either that decision chooses us, or we choose the decision. And every decision is based on a reason we may or may not be aware of.

It's not much of a stretch to say that many of us have our own version of the Eiger, a personal quest that seems impossible and that haunts us as we move through the world. In the realm of the emotional traditions that shape our lives, gaining a map of our emotional landscape is the critical first step to harnessing emotional wealth. Let's look at the first two stages of the ascent that will require us to, first, map our emotional landscape, and second, help us learn how to establish and conduct the type of communication necessary on the ascent.

Stage 1–The Valley Floor

A mountaineer generally begins their trek to the mountain on the valley floor. When we're on the valley floor, we can see the mountain towering above us, but we don't know the exact nature of its hazards yet until we're traversing the ascent. In our emotional lives, the valley floor is a state of unawareness about emotional traditions; we are still playing out the automatic behaviors and narratives about our feelings that we learned from our parents. It is a state of emotional darkness, and we are unable to see the details of what's above us until we begin the slow and challenging climb. Recognizing that we are on the valley floor is the first critical step in our metaphorical ascent of the mountain.

Just as all mountaineers are limited by their carrying capacity—the maximum weight and encumbrance of what they bring to the mountain—many visionaries, leaders and heads of families or organizations don't pay much attention to their emotions because of the pre-existing narratives or emotional traditions they experienced in their own family; they are unaware of their own emotional encumbrance.

For example: maybe you weren't allowed or encouraged to express your emotions from an early age. The discomfort and upset that babies and young children feel often shows up as big and explosive displays of howling and sobbing that your parents might have found dysregulating or embarrassing. How your parents coped with your emotions, as well as their own, could contribute to the emotional traditions you carry into our adulthood.

Just as a mountain climber must develop their preparedness with respect to the conditions of the mountain, anyone embarking on the ascent must prepare for the different conditions they will face. The trek out of the valley floor is the only part of the ascent that must be done alone. This is the time where you begin to map your internal emotional landscape. It requires deep personal inquiry, sitting with some of the most ingrained and most difficult aspects of the emotional traditions that have shaped your life.

Stage II–Base Camp

At the foot of the highest and most climbed peaks on Earth, lies **base camp.** An inherently communal space where teams of climbers aim to summit together, base camp is a staging ground for preparation to assault the peak. Climbers will often spend days or weeks at base camp waiting for optimal conditions, eating together, preparing together, sharing information, trading techniques and bonding with each other. Once they leave base camp, some will not necessarily be traversing the ascent to the summit alone. Others will choose to attempt the summit alone. Their base camp, while not a communal one, remains a preparatory space; equipment is checked, essentials for the summit are packed and the mental and physical conditioning needed for the final push to the summit are undertaken.

For the most difficult and challenging ascents of the highest peaks in the world, professional mountaineers work as a cohesive unit, trusting each other with every traverse over the mountain's hazards. The weather will get harsher up the mountain. Winds will be fierce. Oxygen levels will be lower because the air is less dense than at low elevations. Your legs will feel weaker. You may need another human's body tethered to your rope, anchoring you to the side of a vertical face, and if you fall you fall together.

For an elite climber, communication enables life; it is an essential tool for building trust and common understanding. In our model of the ascent, base camp is where you will learn not merely better communication, but *different* communication. The dialogue conducted both internally and ultimately with others will inform, guide and direct your metaphorical ascent to the mountain's summit.

Eventually, after a difficult and disciplined ascent, you will summit, the prime driver for climbing the mountain. Then what? The summit represents the highest possible version of yourself. From there you can see the ascent you have just undertaken, and the emotional terrain that you have navigated in your ascent. On the summit, there is less oxygen than off the mountain. There are still fierce winds and storms, and the view of the valley below is sometimes shrouded in clouds so thick you can barely see the edge and might face a catastrophic fall.

How do we maintain our position on the summit? Up here we tap into our emotional wealth and human assets. We begin to understand *why* we do what we do, *what* influences our decisions and *how* we react to the changing conditions on the mountain. When we gain this understanding, **we are then able to *choose our behavior* rather than *the behavior choosing us*.** First, we must examine the emotional traditions we inherited from those before us and understand how they define the emotional landscape we carry on the inside.

Questions to ponder:

1. What is a personal quest or challenge in your life that seems rooted in your family?

2. What quest or challenge is so important to you, you know it can only be achieved with passion and commitment that seems beyond what you've ever done?

3. What's your starting point to tackle it?

4. What's your first big milestone toward achieving it?

CHAPTER 4

On the Inside

Emotions are coordinated responses of your thoughts, senses, body responses, and impulses to experiences. They are a critical part of being alive.

Our emotions are not rigorously logical; they don't always follow the rules. As we accumulate experiences, the emotions we have because of those experiences can be extremely powerful, lingering for many years. Sometimes the meaning we attach to those emotions can become a story we tell ourselves, or others.

An *emotional legacy* is an inheritance of emotions—that is, coordinated responses to experiences felt by someone who came before you and passed them down to you, or that you passed down to someone else. For example, every time Ann hears an ambulance siren, she is triggered to feel sadness; her kids observe that growing up and are similarly triggered.

Emotional legacy can be the primary factor of what we become and how we eventually move through the world, determining our relationships with a romantic partner, our relationships with friends, our financial success, our possessions, the quality of our lives, virtually everything that we become.

John du Pont was born on a clear evening on November 22, 1938, in Philadelphia and grew up in the fields of Liseter Hall, a sprawling mansion outside the picturesque downtown of Newton, Pennsylvania, set on 200 lush acres of farmland.

The property was rich with Guernsey cattle, Welsh Ponies, and race horses. Young John was an heir to the DuPont Chemical fortune, one of America's most well-known and wealthy business dynasties.

After graduating from high school, John attended the University of Pennsylvania, the University of Miami and eventually earned a doctorate from Villanova University in 1973. The youngest of four children, his parents divorced when he was two.

Inside the mansion, du Pont was a lonely child. His father was rarely at home and his siblings, who were far older than he, barely acknowledged his existence. The only friend he thought he had was the son of his chauffeur–although, in time, du Pont would find out that his mother had paid the boy to pretend to like him. After the divorce, John was raised by his mother, Jean Liseter Austin, who was said to have seen herself as far superior stock compared to the rest of the world. John's mother's emotional legacy was to raise him often under the care of an estate worker, a Mr. Cherry. Jean was clear with John from a young age that Mr. Cherry was bought and paid for. Throughout John's childhood, Jean reminded John that Mr. Cherry was beneath him.

From the time of the divorce, his father was distant. John idolized his mother and throughout his life they were extremely close. Jean taught John that he must excel and prove his life outside the weight of his inheritance and his family. Any shortcoming would trigger strong, negative emotions related to his self-worth, and how unworthy of love he was.

The outcome was always going to be complicated. Not an athlete himself, John pursued athletics indirectly. He sponsored wrestling teams and invited some of the top Olympic wrestlers in the country to his state-of-the-art training gym that he had built on the Foxcatcher estate. "To become a champion," asserts a plaque on the gym's wall, "you can't just take it to the top. You have to take it over the top."

David Schultz was one of those wrestlers that John invited and their collision would alter both of their lives and families for decades.

David Lesley Schultz was born on June 6, 1959 into a middle-class family. Both he and his younger brother Mark wrestled their way to Gold Medals in wrestling in the 1984 Olympic Games. An overweight child, Dave had been bullied by his classmates, he was called "pudge," and regarded as slow for his dyslexia. It was at David Starr Jordan Middle School that he found wrestling. By the end of high school, David Schultz would go on to win a California State Championship in 1977. California has some of the most elite high-school wrestling in the world–not bad for little Pudge.

By the early 1990s, Schultz was a legend on the mat and an Olympic Champion. Schultz's virtuosity on the mat was only exceeded by his popularity. He was charismatic, knowing how to make everyone around him feel comfortable. A history of being on the business end of schoolyard cruelty and an emotional tradition of craftsmanship in all pursuits had shaped him into a true sportsman.

On a cloudy January afternoon in 1996. Nancy Schultz, Dave's wife, was catching her breath in the living room of the house she, Dave, and their two kids occupied on the Foxcatcher estate. A shot rang out. Rushing to the front door, she peered out just in time to see John du Pont, her and her husband's financial patron, leveling a .38 Caliber Revolver from the rolled down window of his car.

John du Pont screamed like a man possessed, firing again and again at a human mass lying face down on the ground. Du Pont pointed the gun at Nancy and then sped off toward his mansion. Distraught, she ran to and cradled her dying husband. Schultz had been shot three times. *New York Daily News*, during coverage of the Schultz murder, ran the headline: "There's been lots of nuts in this family tree. Generations of scandals, cults, and vicious feuds." It points to a longstanding belief that the wealth of the du Ponts had eventually led to a Frankenstein's monster of destructive values and narcissism. John du Pont's net worth was equivalent to half a\billion of today's dollars when he died in prison in 2010.

Author Jamie Mustard is a writer and artist born into one of the most influential fringe movements in the 1970s: Scientology. The organization raised him in a slum away from his parents and gave him a childhood of abandonment and poverty not far from the hot, concrete slabs that make up downtown Los Angeles. The child of a White father he never knew and a mixed race, Black mother he barely knew, Jamie was rarely if ever in school and was semi-literate until the age of nineteen. Five and a half years later he graduated from The London School of Economics, one of the best universities in the world. What happened?

An unlikely event altered his emotional legacy and his future. At 19, he found his Black grandmother, who lived in a wealthy suburb outside of New York City. She said he was welcome to stay as long as he wanted if he would face his literacy problems. He'd never been able to engage in anything academically with the monkey of poverty, neglect and manipulation clinging to his back. It turned out he was a genius being unfairly destroyed by the emotional legacies of his mother and father, who, for sure, had their own legacies to contend with. And so goes the cycle.

When Jamie arrived in Scarsdale, he was mystified by his grandmother. She had grown up in the segregated South in the small, Black town of Henning, Tennessee, under the crushing laws of Jim Crow. He never understood how she got from there to her large house with a stream running all the way around it set on a lush, private hill. One day he asked her, "How does anyone grow up being told they're less than a person and then end up living so rich?" She told him, "Back then it was different, we had very little, but we had community. Because we could not get full acceptance from White people and our country, we were raised not to get our self-esteem from an external source."

She told him that if he did the same and put one foot in front of the other and never gave up on anything, anything was achievable. She told him to love himself. He was very skeptical, but decided to try. His grandmother changed his emotional legacy.

From Sigmund Freud to Abraham Maslow, thinkers have sifted through the character of the human condition, searching for the fundamental drivers that compel us. What drives us to become a Fortune 500 CEO, or a superstar of sport?

One way to categorize the factors that drive our behavior is to use the Six Human Needs framework developed by motivational speaker Tony Robbins:

- Certainty/Comfort—You meet this need when you feel safe and secure, when you describe your environment as stable and, in many ways, predictable.
    - » Example: Happy family life, financial security, a job that's steady and rewarding.

- Uncertainty/Variety—It's highly likely you want only a certain amount of sameness, and after that, surprises, challenges, excitement, and just a little change in the routine fulfills a need for variety.
    - » Example: Taking a vacation, getting together with an old friend

- Significance—Your desire to feel important, needed, special, and/or respected is universal; when it's met, you feel good all over.
    - » Example: Winning an award at work, being elected to an office in your favorite club.

- Connection/Love—You meet this need when you feel closeness to someone else, bonding with a human or pet, and experiencing shared love.
    - » Example: Friendship, belonging to a church community, a happy marriage.

- Growth—Life is inherently dynamic, and humans naturally feel that. You fulfill the need to experience that rhythm of life when you develop physically, emotionally, intellectually, and/or spiritually.
    - » Example: A DIY project that forces you to learn a new skill, changing your routine at the gym to achieve new goals.

- Contribution—You meet this need when you behave altruistically, going beyond your comfort zone to help others, making a difference to another person or your community

- Example: Volunteering, mentoring, creating an opportunity for someone else to thrive.

We meet these needs in healthy or unhealthy ways. When we identify how we might be meeting our needs in unhealthy ways and see the patterns, we can transform the way we decide to meet our needs into a healthier form.

John du Pont had no sense of belonging or significance. He had no sense of contribution within a limited ability to grow, and very little certainty. He sought variety in destructive ways.

For most of the 300,000 years modern human beings have existed, we have lived in small tribal groups at the mercy of nature. To be shunned or kicked out of the tribe was an urgent threat to our survival; if no one was watching over us, keeping the predators at bay while we slept, or assisting in the daily grind of hunting and gathering, we were simply dead. These needs evolved, and were socially selected, to enable us to better survive the harsh, primeval environment.

We need to use intentional design to meet our six human needs in healthy ways—and that is much of what's covered in upcoming pages of this book.

The emotional legacies of our parents, and their parents, and the generations before them, can impact what we become and how we move through the world. By obtaining a deep understanding of this mechanism we can rewrite the emotional legacy of our family.

As a species primed for situations of environmental uncertainty, scarcity and insecurity, we tend to default to the emotional patterns we were exposed to in our earliest years—a family unit, or company, or tribe is where we replicate what we've experienced. Without deliberate evolution of emotional patterns, they run on autopilot and our futures are shaped by a weak hope that "things will get better tomorrow."

Lee Tamahori directed an astonishing film, *Once Were Warriors*, released in 1994 that was a surprise success. It made the New Zealand director a global sensation and he went on to direct a string of Hollywood hits. In *Once Were Warriors*, Tamahori tells the story of a culture of native people living on the islands of New Zealand called the Māori. It is the intense story of a poor, traumatized and abusive father, descended from great Māori warriors and his wife, a mother trying to protect and help her children navigate the unpredictability and violence of a man she deeply loves. Her oldest 18-year-old son, who is quite handsome with model good looks and beautiful, almost feminine, features, is getting involved with a Māori street gang. Her younger 11-year-old son is going to a local community center every day after school to stay off the streets.

The elder son comes back to their home one day, a humble home located in a slum, with staggeringly detailed tattoos across his face practically destroying his looks. He has undergone getting the ancient tattoos of his esteemed warrior ancestors across his face as a gang ritual—the *moko*, a tattoo that is sacred in the history of the Māori and is said to be the source of their power. At the community center where the younger son is going, an old, distinguished Māori man in a crisp short sleeved shirt and tie is teaching him to wear his powerful history as *internal* values. When the older brother comes home the younger brother is already there. When the younger brother sees his older brother's beautiful—but now mutilated face—he looks at him serenely and says, "I wear my moko on the inside."

We all need to learn to wear our moko on the inside.

Hamish's Story

Hamish is a sixth-generation family member who is now serving as the managing director and Chairman of his 150-year-old family business. On the outside he appears to be happy in his role, but dig a little deeper and on the inside, he is resentful, angry and lonely.

When I was first introduced to Hamish by his son Angus, it didn't take long for me to see past the multiple masks he was wearing. It took several coaching sessions for him to feel emotionally safe with me, but when he did, his guard came down. During our coaching sessions, we uncovered what was driving his feelings of resentment, anger and loneliness. He expressed that he felt he was forced into a role without really having a choice and was carrying large amounts of shame and guilt; one of the many negative emotional family traditions intrinsic to his family.

Hamish shared that when he was ten years old, he listened to his father deliver a speech at the company Christmas party and he remembered feeling incompetent and like a fraud. He was overwhelmed with the idea that one day he would have to do the same and from that day on, he adopted the belief that he'd have to live up to the standards his father had set. The behaviors that Hamish displayed after that fateful Christmas party speech had become part of his everyday life. He rarely spoke his truth, never expressed his emotions and tried to control everything around him, including Angus.

Hamish and Angus both felt the same anguish. They shared the same dread of being the "one" to take over the leadership role in the family business; the feelings of rejecting the birthright of power, influence and responsibility were equal for both men. Totally unaware, Hamish had passed onto his son the feeling that arose from that Christmas party. The energy this carried had such gravitas, that it drove Angus to run away to a sheep farm in Australia where he could be anonymous—a move that led him to abandon his birthright of ownership and leadership.

It was during one of our excursions in Kenya, that Angus told me about the portraits of the past leaders that hung on the wall in the company's office. As a child these photos left him with the expectation that one day he would sit alongside them; a burden so huge that he had grown resentful of the business, his father and all that they represented. It was only when they started working with me and going through the Veritage coaching process—taking on their own ascent, that they began to uncover and understand how they could heal from the wounds that had been causing them so much pain. The dynamic of their relationship shifted from one of hostility, shame and anger, to one of understanding and compassion.

Witnessing Hamish and Angus's transformation has been moving. They both committed to doing the emotional work and now have an open, tender and vulnerable relationship with each other. Not only that, but Hamish has also since stepped down from his Managing Director role and has appointed an external non-family member to take over for him; the very first non-family leader the business has had in seven generations.

Additionally, Angus has taken a leadership role as Chair of the Family Council, and communication amongst the family has improved dramatically.

Both Hamish and Angus have finally accepted their birthright and taken accountability and responsibility for their past behaviors. They now embrace their most authentic selves and are in alignment with each other.

Questions to ponder:

1. Do you avoid feeling your feelings? What are the physical and behavioral signs that you are avoiding or suppressing a feeling?

2. What stories were you told about your feelings as a child that you might be carrying into your adult life?

3. How would you describe your relationship to your feelings and those of others?

4. What is the cost of how you have managed your feelings so far?

5. What do you need to let go of to be able to feel all of your feelings in a healthy way?

CHAPTER 5

The Cult of Family

Can a family be a cult?

The word cult is derived from the Latin word *cultus,* which comes from tilling or cultivation and has its roots in agriculture, to grow things. The word *culture* comes from the same root which is *to care for* or *grow something.* The word cult has come to mean a social group with unusual beliefs and practices that may run counter to traditional beliefs. A cult is not inherently bad, but it's perceived as a deviation from what's acceptable in a given society. With that in mind, a family could seem like a cult.

Given the definition, we could conclude there are good cults and bad cults. Let's start with an example of a good cult that went on to define architecture across neighborhoods in North America—the Roycroft Arts and Craft compound in East Aurora, New York. Roycroft was a social change or reformist community established in 1895 by American artist, writer, and philosopher, Elbert Hubbard. His wife, Alice, was a well-known suffragist and both died upon the sinking of the steamship RMS *Lusitania* by a German U-Boat during the First World War but it was not before this cult would influence how people would live in their domiciles throughout America.

By the time of Elbert's death in 1910 the Roycroft movement and campus in East Aurora was teaming with over 500 workers forwarding the belief and philosophy that handmade furniture architecture was better for human living. The Arts and Crafts movement was a philosophical and artisan protest against mass-production which had been erupting across the world since the 1880s.

The movement had originated in England coming from what was believed to be an extreme decline in production standards as a result of mass-production and machine-based factory manufacturing. This movement would spread from England and across the Western world. Elbert and Alice would be at the center of the mass construction and proliferation of craftsman homes being erected all over America. There is a good chance that you live in one or know many people that do. Influences of the Arts and Crafts movement are everywhere in American cities. These homes at the time were inexpensive to build and are characterized by the beautiful and weather resistant angled roofs, deep overhanging eaves, shingled roofs, wide porches beneath the eaves, a mix of fine woods, large double-hung windows as well as handmade carvings and woodwork.

The philosophy behind the Roycroft movement was that a dwelling would have a serious impact on the life experience of humans. How we live affects who we are. Natural woods, large swaths of natural light and large porches to interact with the community would be more conducive and healthier for human life. The Roycroft Movement and its adherents one could say was a good cult deeply rooted in social reform, women's rights, the protection of children and the abolition of slavery. Famous visitors to the Roycroft campus included Susan B. Anthony, Booker T. Washington, Harry Houdini, Frank Lloyd Wright, Rudyard Kipling, John D. Rockefeller,

Theodore Roosevelt, Harriet Beecher Stowe, Mark Twain and even the king of mass production himself, Henry Ford. In a good cult, individuality and contribution or celebration, freedom of information and physical freedom are a combined strength working toward good. A good cult might well engender meeting all six needs for a human. This is what was experienced by the artisans living on the Roycroft compound.

Let's take a look at how a bad cult operates. Seeking to captivate and control the lives of their members, bad cults will often use the information adherents have access to, the emotions they feel and the thoughts they have about their emotions to manipulate members' behavior. This could look like control of information through compartmentalization, or even banning outside information entirely such as books, popular media, TV shows and music to narrow the knowledge a member has available to them; contradictory information that might make a person question the leader.

Some cults deploy controls over members to elicit a feeling of dependency on the cult. This might look like control of their living environment, what clothes they wear, the food they eat, their speaking, or who they form relationships with. The word brainwashing is typically used where cults are concerned, the idea being that a member's thoughts are re-written with new ones like some B-Movie version of *Total Recall.* In fact, it's more that members internalize cult ideology by picking up on the behavior cues from the other members. Using the cult's specific language system or following the cult's determination of reality as "the truth," so they can be thought of as good members.

In short, a bad cult might provide an environment to meet all six needs in an unhealthy way.

In any family with a negative emotional legacy, destructive emotional control looks like you would expect. A nonacceptance and narrowing of the "acceptable" range of feelings a member can express, or redefining them as toxic, even sinful, or wrong encourages dependency on the cult for personal validation. Bad cults instill fear in members for questioning or leaving the cult, promoting unworthiness and guilt while others teach thought-stopping techniques, passed off as "centering" or "mindfulness" that stop healthy anger, questioning, or homesickness. Love-bombing followed by shunning, or degradation of junior members of a family or group, causes extreme highs and lows within and creates a toxic culture.

Gaslighting, now used as a cliché, is the hallmark of bad cults. Named after a 1944 film noir about a husband trying to drive his wife insane to keep her from uncovering his murder of an opera singer, gaslighting involves using manipulation to make a person question their perception of reality and become dependent on those manipulating them.

Do the above traits remind you of your family or a family you know? Do you think there is any planet where these traits ensure your family legacy? It is very unlikely they will. However, this kind of emotional control is common among families all over the world, of every kind. While it's hard to imagine mind-control and indoctrination operating inside normal families, it happens all the time.

Families with entrenched cultic dynamics are such a part of the cultural landscape we see them all over popular culture. In the American TV series *Succession*, Logan Roy's emotions dictate the behavior of every family member around him. He is, at times, so volatile and unpredictable that his children often triangulate—with him and against each other—to regulate their emotions and stabilize themselves. The Roy family is effectively held hostage by Logan Roy's emotions. His children can't freely build their own individual identities because their survival is entirely reliant on their ability to anticipate and manage Logan's emotions. This state of enmeshment—where the boundaries between individuals are undefined—exists in many families around the world.

Children in such a family tread lightly through the emotional minefield its dynamics create. If a child doesn't see their father asserting his own happiness as equally important in the family, they grow up to be people-pleasers too. Pleasing, and not reason, or critical thinking, or love and care, can destroy a family. An interesting and common theme among heads of destructive cults is they rarely if ever have a succession plan. David Koresh and his Branch Dividians in Waco, Texas, Jim Jones and his People's Temple and Charles Manson and his family all did not have a succession plan as a result of the divine grandiosity of the leader.

One thing I find consistently in working with families to understand their emotional traditions is, **how we manage money is how we manage relationships.** The root cause of this pattern in our lives stems from how our family created values around money. If you think back on your parents or caretakers, how was their relationship with money? Were they buried under a mountain of bills, under pressure to make ends meet every month? Were they frivolous with their money, spending it on fads and trends that would quickly be replaced by other fads and trends? Were they cash-comfortable but so restrictive with spending that the family lived well below their means to be ready for some imminent and inevitable emergency that never came?

These behaviors, and others like them, communicate a set of values around money that could transfer onto us without our even being aware of it. And they don't just show up in how we manage money, they show up in how we manage our relationships.

There are three components to family wealth:

Financial capital. This is the tangible wealth a family possesses—assets like money, property, investments, and ownership in businesses. Financial capital provides the resources to support lifestyle, fund opportunities (like education or entrepreneurship), and create generational security. It's often the most visible form of wealth but also the most volatile without strong foundations in the other two forms.

Human Capital. This is the sum of individual capabilities, values, health, and personal development within the family. It includes emotional intelligence, self-awareness, adaptability, and the ability to make wise decisions. Human capital shapes how family members engage with opportunities and challenges—and whether they use financial capital wisely or destructively.

Human capital can also present a negative risk to a business or to the group when a person's negative beliefs, especially beliefs about money such as shame or guilt around the family's wealth, are amplified. Next Generations, when they inherit the family's money, might develop a negative belief around money because they haven't built anything themselves.

Social Capital. This refers to the value created by relationships—trust, networks, shared values, and mutual support. On the individual level, it's about personal relationships that offer emotional and practical support. On the collective level, it includes the family's reputation, community ties, and ability to collaborate across generations or social systems.

A family might have a financial trust that funds a child's education, or a business passed from one generation to the next. If t hat child, as they grow into a young adult and inherit the family's wealth, has developed emotional resilience and purpose-driven goals, they are more likely to sustain and grow that wealth. That same adult may gain access to influential networks or support in times of crisis—benefiting everyone connected to them.

Another family might have no financial trust, or their assets are poorly managed—leaving behind debts and unresolved conflicts. The child grows into a young adult who inherits the chaos without developing emotional resilience or clear purpose. They are more likely to mismanage resources, repeat destructive patterns, or experience burnout. Without strong ties or a supportive reputation, that same adult may find themselves isolated in times of crisis—leaving both themselves and their wider family more vulnerable.

For most families, it's a messy mix of both gifts and gaps. A family may pass down some financial assets—perhaps a home, a business, or modest savings—but these can be entangled with debt, conflict, or unclear expectations.

Some family members develop emotional awareness, resilience, and a sense of direction—while others carry unprocessed trauma, reactive behaviors, or feel stuck in inherited roles. The social network may include both strong, loyal relationships and strained, dysfunctional ties—trust may coexist with resentment, and support may come inconsistently.

Henrick's Story

Stanley, Henrick, and Sarah were siblings, born four years apart. Growing up in the rural Midwest in what is known in America as "fly-over" country, theirs is a classic immigrant story of becoming the bedrock of the American business community. Their father, Arnold, was a driven and industrious man who wanted to build something both he and his family could be proud of. Coming from a long line of potato farmers in Ireland, Arnold's father worked hard, yet never seemed to achieve wealth, which became how Arnold measured success.

Arnold had witnessed his father work hard, from the break of dawn and into dusk, and even though he was a hard worker, was unable to achieve the financial wealth he wanted. This will not happen to me, Arnold told himself. So, with that belief he set out to build what would end up being a very successful business in real estate development. His modest early ventures into building homes and then selling them to a growing population grew into building communities, apartment buildings and shopping centers. Slowly his wealth grew and so did his kids, Henrick and Sarah.

Henrick is tall, lanky and owing to his full set of red hair, was teased and bullied in school. As he shared in our coaching sessions, he always felt socially awkward and even though he was emotionally connected and could see things others could not, he made the decision early in life that hiding was the "safe" thing for him to do. Henrick shared how he would hide his emotions and feelings because it was considered a sign of weakness, and he wouldn't be teased for "being soft and girl-like."

Hiding became his way through life. Yet Henrick desperately wanted to be seen. On the inside, he felt being seen was too risky. If others ever did see him, he would be ridiculed and shamed because being himself was being fundamentally, irreparably wrong. Henrick quickly realized that if he was "good"—meaning that he performed the way others expected him to—he would be acknowledged, a seemingly safe way to be seen. So, his pattern became a performance of being 'the good son.'

Henrick's family had done all the right things when it came to succession planning. They had engaged with the top professionals and financial institutions in crafting the legal and operational structure for the transition but still Henrick felt something was missing. They could not put a finger on what that missing piece was until one day, over lunch, Henrick heard me speak about the biggest risk a family business faces: **Behavioral Risk**. The risk of human emotion present in the system.

What Henrick was seeking so desperately was to be accepted for how he was and yet his emotional conditioning kept him from attaining this desire. He realized that, to understand why he was living a life of hiding and self-suppression, he needed to look at how emotions had been modeled for him by others throughout his life. Henrick chose to speak with his father.

Arnold had accumulated massive wealth, and his new measurement of success was a healthy, united family. He had read many stories of families that amassed massive wealth, more than he had, and yet had failed in the end game. Their families had collapsed under the pressure of the father's success. In many cases, the father had failed as a father because he over-valued the material and financial contribution to the family's resources, often neglecting or even feeling incapable of contributing to the family's emotional resources. Arnold's encounter with this pattern in other fathers left him feeling a deep desire not to fall into the trap many fathers had: Achieving great financial wealth yet leaving an emotionally bankrupt family.

By choosing to address his behavioral risk and actions by speaking with his father, Henrick took the first step out of hiding and stepped into the light to face what was missing in their succession plan. This was the beginning of Henrick's visibility to himself, his family and the community around him. Building what I call a *safe space* to talk through his internal reality with his father, he now fully accepts himself and sees the beauty he brings to his family and those he serves.

He has now taken over the family business and has grown it even beyond where Arnold had left it. Henrick is no longer afraid and has chosen to be seen for who he is.

In the journey to develop their system of emotional governance, every family must uncover their past emotional traditions. Many families come from a long line of not expressing one's feelings, treading on eggshells for fear of being seen, and paralyzed with fear of conflict. Many families would rather avoid awkward conversations than find the backbone to have them.

With a system of emotional governance in place, families can feel emotionally safe to share what they are feeling and thinking and to take accountability for their actions. We can design new emotional behaviors—good cult behaviors—if we have the courage and commitment to change the past and design the future.

Here are four steps to assist you on the path:

The Four Domains of Emotional Intelligence

Each of these can help you face any crisis with lower levels of stress, less emotional reactivity and fewer unintended consequences.

- **Self-Awareness:** Finding individual Safe Space

- **Self-Management:** Using Safe Space to create emotional governance

- **Social Awareness:** Relational and familial Safe Space
- **Relationship Management:** Operating with a set of agreed-upon guiding principles and boundaries.

Has your family codified, or listed its values? They could be spending time together during major holidays, assets like a home that you share, and participating in volunteer work that benefits the community.

Let's look at an example of a family with a power and positive emotional legacy despite the harshest of human conditions. Sir Herbert Holt of Canada is the most successful businessman in the last century that you have never heard of. He came to North America as a modest civil engineer in the 1880s, in his late teens—he came with no station, nor money to speak of. Ultimately, he built what is now known as Hydro-Québec, which powers all of Montreal, Quebec and even exports power to the United States. Holt also built the most significant portion of the Canadian Railroad, the Royal Bank of Canada, and was knighted by King George V in 1915.

Sir Herbert married Jessie Paton in 1890 and had three sons. Holt and his wife taught their children values of hard work, to always help others, to not discriminate based on class or color and to shun entitlement. A hundred years later the Holt fortune lives on in Jessie and Herbert's great grandson, Brendan Holt Dunn who has received and lives by the values of hard work, contribution and harnessing the power of people from diverse places and culture in the workplace.

Jim Warren Jones was born May 31, 1931, in the farming hamlet of Crete, Indiana. His father, James Thurman Jones, was addled by chronic asthma, the aftereffect of a German gas attack on the Western Front during World War I. His thirty-dollar monthly federal pension brought the family up short, leaving the tasks of providing to Jim's mother, Lynette. Haughty and self-important, she self-styled as Lynetta. Her maiden name was Putnam.

Lynette Putnam wasn't like other girls. She was taught to think she was destined for great things to bestow upon the world. She was born of privilege, carried a masculine veneer, and was unafraid of defying social order. As Lynette would describe her own life, she embodied the folk hero spirit of John Dillinger, facing down depression-era bank cartels, and while weathering the drunken cruelty of her broken husband, gave birth to a son in the throes of mythic delirium.

Despite any hardship Lynette was a legend in her own mind. As a result of marrying down and her own life not becoming what she imagined, Lynette decided she would raise the most important man of the twentieth century. Her emotional legacy would become a horror show.

The Jones family was so poor they lived in a shack without plumbing gifted to them by relatives. The ultimatum came down from the family that owned the house: She would have to do what most people do—get a job. As a result, between her work and her husband's frequent hospitalizations because of The Great War, Jim was left to fend for himself.

By the time he was twelve, Jim was submerged in his own inner world, friendless and marked by religion and death. His six human needs were never met. Du Pont was resource rich; Jones was resource poor. The ugly future was the same.

By the 1950s, as a result of his mother's aggrandizement, neglect as well as her religious nature, Jim decided to establish himself as a Methodist preacher. The Black Civil Rights movement was boiling over in America, and the wounds of racial segregation were festering in almost every corner of the American South. Jim was in his early twenties.

Jim was also living life on the edge. With an emotional tradition of being an outsider, he enthusiastically invited Blacks to join his congregation at a time when America had turned its back on its own history. The Christian establishment protested by dismissing him from his position in the church, further turning him away from the mainstream.

Jim's aloneness and strangeness was always his ally, we see once again a severely damaged boy-man cloaked in a mission of good. By 1956 Jim built his People's Temple, an offbeat church of progressive Christian spiritualists who preached a doctrine of racial integration, cultural overthrow, and Marxist utopia. He was always comfortable being different and going against the grain.

Jim embraced Black America before The Civil Rights Movement. The growth of his church was fueled by the ever-growing numbers of an otherwise alienated and degraded Black population. Over the next twenty years Jim's congregation would swell to over 2,500 members.

In November 1978, members of the Guyana Defense Force trekked deep into the festering jungles of its small South American Nation. The soldiers closed in on Jonestown, the offbeat commune Jim had carved out as a community for his followers in the muggy Guyanese jungles in 1974. One soldier later described his difficulty finding footing, he tripped over logs every other step. As the soldiers approached the outskirts of Jonestown, where the jungle had been cleared, it was obvious to the soldiers what the logs actually were—there were human bodies everywhere.

Jim Jones was found lying on his back on the raised stage in the Jonestown pavilion, a gunshot wound to his head. Somehow, he had also taken the lives of 909 people—many of them the elderly and children. Jim had recorded the death ritual on audiotape. At the end of the tape, he concludes, with the voices of children screaming in the background: "We didn't commit suicide; we committed an act of revolutionary suicide protesting the conditions of an inhumane world." Like the Roycroft movement, the doctrine of the cult was rooted in a genuine desire for social reform; both cults would probably agree that humans needed to live differently, with greater intention. However, the follow-through of that doctrine was directly shaped by the emotional legacies inherited by its founders.

The Roycroft movement was rooted in the emotional legacy of Elbert Hubbard. His doctrine had also been the improvement of an American society for Black people after slavery, and equal rights for all. In 1899 Elbert had written *A Message to Garcia,* one of the most successful essays in history. Being printed 40 million times, it told the story of a young soldier who delivered a message despite impossible odds as parable and metaphor for getting something done regardless of the barriers that life presents to us.

Consider the contrast between Hubbard's good "cult" and Jim Jones's People's Temple. Both aim for a sense of transcendence, but only one offers "no alternative." With Jim Jones, as long as the member abides by the values, codes and ideals of the cult, they believe they will be protected from an otherwise chaotic and hostile world. There is a sense of belonging, but it's wrapped in chains.

By the time you are born, the emotional legacy of your family has already been established and passed down to you. If your parents don't have awareness of their own emotional patterns, they pass those patterns onto you. Negative cultic family emotional legacies cause vulnerability through creating discomfort that, overlooked or unexamined, can provoke addiction to the destruction of self, and the family. This is true no matter how resourced your family is. There are emotional dynamics at play that have existed since before your birth and you will be affected by them. Building an understanding of those dynamics is the first crucial step in changing your family's emotional legacy.

For example, a family that allows entitlement to run rampant creates a dangerous emotional legacy and it can even be deadly. The streets of Hollywood are painted with the blood of movie producers and actors who had awards, acclaim, and money but not the emotional structure in their lives that would enable them to experience success in a healthy way.

A stone's throw away from Hollywood, the streets of South Central LA are painted with the blood of gang members and their children. Young people join gangs for the same reason people join cults—as a substitute for family. If you want to ensure the future of your family no matter your resources, you need to ensure the emotional needs of that family.

The emotional needs of a family look the same no matter where we come from. Under the current authoritarian regime in North Korea, the punishment of dissenters and lawbreakers lasts for up to three generations. Imagine being legally sanctioned or even exiled for the thoughts and actions of your grandparents. Humans are directly impacted by the environmental conditions and traumatic events experienced by previous generations. Famed Psychologist Gabor Maté supports the idea of biological generational impact, describing that the modern world we live in increases the stresses that impact pregnant mothers. A codified family legacy will mitigate the effect.

Cults operate by conditioning how we relate to our own emotions. Most often any emotions that are deemed as threats to the leader, or the cult, are negatively labelled and demonized. One of the most common responses to emotions that are considered "bad" or "wrong" is to suppress them. When we bury our emotions deep inside, they tend to get stored in the body in the form of physiological and psychological effects. Eventually they might even "leak" in unexpected ways. Anxiety and depression, generalized worry, health problems, stress and overwhelm, addiction can all be the results of suppressed emotions. We often wait for life-altering events such as a death, a diagnosis, a graduation, or a marriage to allow ourselves to show emotions. Showing, or not showing emotions is a choice.

Someone in a cult, family or other, has to build a new emotional tradition to fill the space the connection to the cult provided. Navigating our emotions is an internal and panoramic process and can be done through a framework of emotional governance—a framework to manage emotions so they are a benefit and not a detriment to you and the community you're a part of. Building that framework begins with an awareness about your beliefs, behaviors, feelings and the stories you have around those feelings.

A tool that I developed to help people become more competent with this, is the acronym ACT: **Awareness, Choice** and **Transformation**. It is a sustainable process at the crux of emotional governance.

In **Awareness**, you need to recognize that you are in a state I call the Land of Familiar. I explore this concept later in the book. You need to ask yourself, "Is this behavior that I'm engaging in an automatic, default response?" and if so you then need to ask, "Does this behavior serve me and where I'm going?"

The **Choice** is to act differently. If you want to change your behavior to something else, you have to believe that "different" means moving away from pain. You have to respond differently to what you encounter, in how you treat others, and most importantly in how you treat yourself.

Both steps lead to **Transformation**, the start of change and the start of moving into a new future where you relate differently with awareness of what's going on internally for yourself and others.

Given that humans can be masters at justifying their own behavior, it can be helpful to work alongside a professional who can serve as a guide on the journey, because once we are able to have self-awareness, we are then faced with the truth of our emotions, and in turn the choice to embrace, learn and transform. We either break the patterns, or the patterns break us.

Acting is the first step to leaving the bad cult behind.

Education Day

The very first part of the Veritage coaching process is what we refer to as "education day." It's a structured, half-day experiential workshop designed to allow a family to learn some of the tools and concepts we use in the coaching process. Most importantly, it allows the family to get a taste of what Safe Space could feel like should they choose to work with us.

Time and again, at the end of the education day, family members comment, "it was really nice to truly speak and have the conversations we had over the last few hours," or "I wish we could speak like that with each other all the time." We all want to feel emotionally safe expressing ourselves with those we care about. Yet we have not been taught how to, because we are stuck in our Land of Familiar; and we are afraid of the consequences of speaking how we truly feel and sharing what we really think because in the past we may have been ridiculed, shamed, or punished for it.

To allow families and groups to experience and feel Safe Space, we ask the participants to share how they feel about money, as well as the beliefs they have about it, and most importantly the impact these feelings/beliefs have on how they behave with money or deal with it.

Here are a couple of examples of what we have heard. Three next generation family members, all in their late twenties and early thirties, currently working alongside their siblings in the family business.

Carrie shared how her friends make comments that she can pay for everything because her family is rich. This leads her to think she is only liked for the money her family has and the success of the family business. Carrie feels disappointed, unloved and questions if she can trust her friends to be with her for who she is and not her family's wealth. Her belief is, "people only want to hang out with me for the money and good times." As a result, Carrie keeps herself small and defaults to paying for everyone.

Margaret shared that she was being given money to buy a house. Immediately she thought to herself, "I am spoiled." Feelings of guilt, sadness, not being good enough and being fundamentally unworthy of such a gift began to influence her. The internalized beliefs are "I don't deserve the money," and "I should not need help from anyone in the form of money." Margaret's behavior has been to reject the money and not share how she feels about money and the family business.

Jeremy shared how his friends call him a spoiled brat and that he feels, because his family is rich, he has no real issues. Jeremy thought, "having money makes me a bad person." He felt sad, unrelatable, frustrated and isolated. He believed that "people always jump to conclusions about me before they even know me," and so he chronically over-works, to the detriment of his health, trying to prove how not spoiled he is and that he does have a work ethic. Perhaps Jeremy's biggest struggle is that he hides his feelings and thoughts and as a result doesn't allow others to know his true self. "No one really knows me," he shared, "including myself. I feel like a stranger within myself and am unhappy and lonely."

At the end of this particular education day, where Carrie, Margaret and Jeremy shared their suppressed feelings, their parents asked me if there was a guarantee I can give them for engaging with me in building a Safe Space and emotional governance of the family. The response was not what they were expecting. I asked them, "what do you think will happen to these kids emotionally when they inherit hundreds of millions of dollars in the form of a business and everything that entails?"

I told them that if these feelings, beliefs and behaviors about money their children were carrying were not addressed and transformed by design, these were guaranteed to get in the way of the family legacy. The feelings of guilt, isolation and not deservedness would self-sabotage any succession process. They would contribute to added pressure of taking over the ownership and running of the business. If we don't address the emotions of the past, they will leak all over the present and impact the future.

BANG! You're Dead.

How do you react when certain feelings are triggered? No doubt some of those reactions cause discomfort, in others and in yourself. Some of them might even be ugly. Once you acknowledge this, then you can ask if you felt you had a choice to react differently, would you? By choosing to respond differently—in an honest, constructive way—you can transform your relationship to the emotion if emotion is something you have a hard time experiencing from others.

In my work I often play a game called "Bang! You're dead." It's an exercise with family businesses where I encourage my clients to imagine that something has taken them out of the world. How do they imagine their family will deal with the loss? Does the family move on okay, or does it completely fall apart? How could individual members be affected by the death? Do they even know?

These are questions worth asking ourselves, because emotional issues surrounding death arise in all of us. The practicalities that follow are one thing, but the feelings that arise from the unspoken words are the hardest parts to navigate, and only further highlights the problems that arise when people don't live, speak or share their truth. As parents we are responsible for creating a powerful emotional legacy for our children, so despite what we've experienced ourselves as a child, we have the choice to continue or end a perpetual cycle.

You end the cycle because you choose a different outcome; if you want different you have to become different. The fundamental work that we do is much like the Step-Work in Alcoholics Anonymous, or Codependents Anonymous—a step-by-step series of intentional internal changes that, through repetition, become cellular; you have to embody them in your actions.

The first step in this process is to catch yourself in your negative patterns, without judgment, and then ask yourself, "What am I doing in this moment?" then, "What do I need to do *differently*?"

My core belief in any situation wherein I felt triggered into my unhelpful patterns was, "It's always my fault." I had to learn over time, and through lots of repetition, to catch myself in those moments and be able to say to myself, "Maybe it's not my fault, maybe it's the client projecting their pain and I'm interpreting it as my fault."

Whatever the internalized narrative looks like for you, it's important to know that even when the step-work becomes internalized, the things we have dealt with will continue to show up, sometimes when we least expect it. The negative beliefs are still inside of you and with awareness, you don't have to give them power.

Death presents some valuable questions that we could all do with asking ourselves; it is a pivotal moment in which a family's future may be determined.

For families struggling to manage resources, emotions seem irrelevant given the stark physical reality of the economic hardship that might have been incurred by the loss of an earner. In either case, this is where emotions matter more than anything, because it is the moment in which your family's future may be determined. Do you go on to create a powerful emotional legacy for your children despite the loss you've experienced? Or do you look at emotions as secondary and perpetuate what can be an endless cycle of dysfunction and pain?

Giovanni's Story

Giovanni is the founder of a multibillion-dollar empire and has been driven to succeed from an early age; a motivation that came from his need and desire to support all six of his siblings. He wanted help to prepare his five children, then in their 20s and 30s, to take a role in the decision-making process within the business.

As I started to work with the children and the chairman of the board it became apparent that there was a deep-rooted culture of judgment and very little accountability. I recall having a coaching session scheduled with the chairman where he turned up thirty minutes late. What I found fascinating was that the children, with whom I had a meeting right after, assumed that I would start their meeting thirty minutes late because of the chairman's tardiness.

When he casually showed up, I politely told him we had thirty minutes left of the scheduled sixty-minute time slot. He looked at me in complete disbelief, to which I responded, "The standards we are willing to walk past are the standards we accept."

Quick aside: I know a middle-class family that always ate dinner together, but it was often late because dad worked late. In this family, the children assumed that no one could eat until the "head of the household" showed up.

As I started working with Giovanni, I began to unpack the root cause of the issue. Being the oldest child, Giovanni learnt from a young age that the only way to get his mother's attention, approval or love was to "perform." Performing meant being the "rescuer" and taking the blame for his siblings whenever they got in trouble, thereby taking away the opportunity for them to take accountability for their actions. Over time, Giovanni unconsciously made the emotional connection that for him to receive love, attention or approval he must "save and rescue" others; a pattern that he continued into his adult life.

This emotional connection is what I like to call a *false equation*. For example, I have known clients to establish a pattern whereby they associate love with need, yet the two can live exclusively of one another. You can be loved and not needed, and you can be needed and not loved. For Giovanni, he believed that by performing as the rescuer, he would get attention, which he equated to feeling loved.

Giovanni had continued playing out this false equation with his own five children and the chairman of his board. The consequence for everyone is that none of them ever had to take accountability for anything, not even keeping the time of an appointment. This culture had become hugely problematic for Giovanni and made a successful succession plan impossible. His false equation had been playing out for so long that none of his children were qualified or even had the capability to take over.

Their houses had been bought for them, their jobs were given to them, and they were financially taken care of. Other than occasionally showing their face at the office, they had zero responsibility. Despite Giovanni's desire to prepare them to one day take over the business, none of them had ever had to learn the skills needed to do so and instead were automatically given a seat on the board. An analogy I sometimes use is: Would you let someone who had only just passed their driving license race in a F1 Grand Prix?

As a result, the children felt intense pressure and reacted negatively. Instead of sharing their concerns with their father, they turned inwards and judged themselves, blaming the executives and their father, who conversely felt he was providing them with an amazing opportunity.

Before any progress could be made collectively, I worked with Giovanni on an individual level to help him understand the consequences of his false equation and the impact it was having on his relationships, and the future potential of the business. Giovanni's pattern was that, in donning the cape and saving everyone else he was repeating the same rescuer pattern with both the chairman and his kids. It was tearing his family apart. He could keep repeating this pattern and break his family and the company, or he could ACT. We break the patterns, or the patterns break us.

To move forward, Giovanni had to make some difficult decisions and engage in some uncomfortable and honest conversations with his children, and in turn they had to do the same. For some, this meant admitting to their father that they had no interest in the business or being involved in the operations.

Once we had opened the communications channels, we were then able to put a framework in place that everyone felt aligned with and that held them accountable to a set of guiding principles. Since the development and implementation of this, Giovanni has created a professional board and put mechanisms in place to protect his children as they continue to be passive shareholders.

All relationships, families and businesses have a culture that they have created either willing or unwillingly. This culture is often based on the false equations that the leaders or the individuals set from the outset. Always remember the standard you are willing to walk by is the standard you are willing to accept.

Questions to ponder:

1. What are some of the behavioral patterns you notice in your relationship and or family?

2. How have you contributed to these behavioral patterns?

3. What are some of your own false equations—emotional patterns that operate by connecting a behavior with a narrative that justifies it—that are impacting your relationships?

4. What type of culture do you want to create for the future of your family?

5. What is currently standing in the way of you creating this future for your family?

CHAPTER 6

Impostor

We all know what addiction is. In our mind's eye, we could see the gambler in Las Vegas who haunts the Blackjack table and doesn't know when to call it quits—as if each trick is guaranteed to be the perfect combination of skill and luck. We could possibly picture the drug-addicted old hippie roughing it in New York and we would almost certainly feel some judgment as if the addiction is evidence of a weakness of character, mental illness, or flimsy morals.

In reality, less obvious, and ostensibly harmless, addictions are common.

Hungarian-Canadian physician and author, Gabor Maté writes in his seminal book *In The Realm of Hungry Ghosts: Close Encounters with Addiction*, "It is impossible to understand addiction without asking what *relief* (emphasis mine) the addict finds, or hopes to find, in the drug or the addictive behaviour." Hidden beneath the array of behaviors we call addiction is the compulsive pursuit of a feeling that we tell ourselves will help us escape another feeling.

The word impostor comes to us from the Latin word *impositus*, meaning "to place upon, impose upon, or deceive." When we become addicted to a substance, or a way of thinking and feeling, we are imposing upon ourselves—we become impostors. There is one thing we all possess as humans from our earliest days as children, something that is partially imposed upon us by the emotional traditions in our families and the social reality in which we live, and also partially created and shaped by the stories we tell ourselves about ourselves: an identity.

Identity comprises our actions, beliefs, and behaviors. It is how we show up to those around us. It comprises our values, our priorities, what we treasure and how we desire to be seen. Our identity is mutable, something that we mold and shape again and again throughout our lives. Like Michelangelo, the Italian Renaissance sculptor and architect drawing out a timeless and ideal human figure from within a solid block of marble, we might spend many years carving and shaping our identity. As we grow older, our identity could become so hyper-realized and inflexible that we limit our ability to adapt to the constantly changing reality around us. In this way, maintaining a hardened and rigid identity can be a form of addiction. It can trap us in an uncompromising cycle of despair, isolation and pain. Our identity can become an impostor.

The Runaway and The Rebel

In the great novels of Charles Dickens and Horatio Alger, literature, film and other popular media are consistently bursting not only with examples of emotional traditions that drive fictional characters to act, but also with stories of addiction. It is an experience that is universal and pervasive affecting every culture in history. From the Greek myth of Narcissus, who becomes captivated by his own reflection, to the modern tabloid, we are inundated with stories of addiction that have taken fictional characters from the dizzying heights of power to a meteoric fall from grace—and sometimes back again.

When we over-identify with our pain, shame, anger, and hurt, it can become an addiction as fierce as any addiction to alcohol, sex, or drugs. Whatever narrative we attach to our addiction, our driver is the feelings that emerge from regulating the discomfort signals of our nervous system. The temporary relief we find through addiction, whatever it may be, could make us increasingly dependent on whatever behaviors serve that addiction. These behaviors, even if harmful to us, become our new normal and we tell ourselves stories to maintain that new normal.

Sometimes, we might feel as though we are owed something and that it should become a part of us. We might feel entitled to the stories we tell ourselves about why we behave the way we do, or about the feelings we have. My addiction was to my feelings of shame. I felt entitled to it. Shame was my identity and my normal.

Identity Is the Biggest Addiction

For many years, I felt my life had to be hard. Any time *hard* wasn't happening—whenever my life felt like it was getting too easy—I had to go make it hard. I had to bring shame into my life.

I grew up feeling emotionally unsafe in my home, at school and within myself. My mother was constantly reminding me I was born on the wrong side of the tracks, giving me mixed messages about what love and connection were. The basic message I got drilled into my young head and psyche was "It's my fault and I will be punished because it's my fault." This created inside me a foundation of what was to become my Imposter, based on shame and a chronic feeling of not belonging.

From the age of five years my mother started to abuse me sexually. Throughout my childhood I was treated as her surrogate husband when my father was not around. He worked hard and was constantly away on business. My mother was lonely, and she made her young child, me, her only source of comfort.

When my father would return home from his trips, I would get a physical beating because my mother would tell him what occurred during his absence—what I did wrong. My father was a jealous man and instead of protecting me from the predatory behavior of his wife, I got his rage.

This constant cycle of behavior in my home formed my core belief, "it's my fault" and I will be punished because it's my fault." It's my fault that my mother is lonely, it's my fault I cannot stop the abuse, it's my fault my father does not protect me… *it's my fault.*

This belief was the contributor to my behavioral risk: That life had to be hard—in all areas. Business, relationships—both friendships and intimate ones. Money especially, it all had to be hard, it had to be a struggle. If I was not struggling, I did not deserve whatever I was achieving.

Shame became my friend. It was what I sought out constantly. It was my emotional tradition as well as my addiction. It was all I knew from six years old. Shame for wanting to be loved, shame for being loved in this perverse way by my mother and father, through the abuse and beatings.

The message I learned about love from my childhood was that it was only sexual and shameful.

Once, during the holiday season in Vancouver, British Columbia, I was in a dark place, drinking heavily and seriously considering ending my life. Somehow, I had the wherewithal to call a friend and share what was going on with me. He invited me to go for a walk with him, and as we walked through the chilly streets of a Canadian winter, he shared a way of thinking about my behavior that I would never forget.

He explained to me that as our experiences accumulate throughout our lives, we attach meaning to them and we often create equations between our feelings, our desires and our outcomes. Sometimes we create false equations between how we feel what we want, and what we think is necessary for us to have that desire met. Sometimes we create false equations between how we feel, what we want to avoid and what we think is necessary for us to avoid that thing. For me, my false equation had been:

Love = Sex = Connection = Shame

I didn't form this false equation consciously. It formed for me based on how love, sex, shame and connection were introduced to me in childhood. Because my earliest sexual experiences were distorted by my parents, with strong feelings of shame attached to sex and love, I had come to believe that love was shameful; the very feeling of love or wanting to be loved was shameful.

I grew up seeking relationships that would inevitably shame me, or I would shame my partners. Shaming verbally through humor that hurts , or emotionally by withdrawing or avoidance.

This was my imposter, and it got in the way of my finding joy, ease and peace in my relational life especially for a long time. Even at times today, when I get triggered, my default at first goes to "it's my fault and I will be punished." It is because of the work I have done on my journey of self-awareness and personal development that I am able to recognize my imposter when he shows up and with compassion ask him to leave the space in my mind, the place he was a tent for so long.

What I experienced in my childhood and adolescence, and the emotional tradition I internalized, created in me a set of lies that I used to protect my impostor, lies about my self-worth that kept my impostor alive. Even once I had reached a level of financial success, I couldn't seem to break through. If I wasn't fully accepting myself then how can I ever accept wealth?

Because of the boundary violations I had experienced, I didn't feel safe. To keep these lies working to keep my identity alive, I needed to be in control of everything. It took me a long time to process and understand that, for me, shame was my addiction and a core foundational piece of my impostor—built on the emotional traditions I created, the ones I inherited from my parents and the lies I told myself about myself. What I was given, or not given, emotionally expanded to become part of my emotional make up contributing to the identity I built.

There are three fundamental lies of identity: **the lies we tell ourselves about ourselves, the lies we tell ourselves about relationships and the lies we tell ourselves about money.** All of these lies are supported by our emotional traditions and the addictions and patterns that play out in our lives—patterns that get our needs met in unhealthy ways. If I told you to picture Steve Buscemi, you would likely see his unconventional looks and anxious energy that often saw him cast as the nervous oddball criminal of a *Fargo* or *Reservoir Dogs*. Like a Hollywood character actor, we can typecast ourselves in a role that we know how to play all too well.

If our traditions around wealth, or other ways of meeting our needs, are unhealthy then we have to build new and healthy traditions, or the unhealthy familiar patterns will crush us. The ascent is about identifying those three lies which are the foundation of our default identity, and transforming them by building our **designed identity**, just as we would design a house or a business. A designed identity is exactly what it sounds like, an identity we choose to create with awareness and intention, and in order to create it we have to transform our three lies into truths.

For me, "it's always my fault," became "I'm a gift." While "money is for others," became, "I am treasured." Finally, "so if I make money, I can fit in with them and I won't be rejected," transformed into, "my value creates my wealth." My need to create safety for myself through control transformed into allowing things to unfold naturally.

Grieving the Loss of the Life You Knew

Often, the biggest addiction that visionaries and leaders of groups have is to their identity. It might be built on a narrative of visionary sacrifice, actions, beliefs, and behaviors that revolve around their mission, whether it is being an effective leader or operating a business. Many founders who have built businesses or organizations had their operation rely on them for decades. It is how they see themselves—the CEO, the chair, the leader of the company; the one on whose shoulders the company legacy depends. Others have relied on them for so long that to ever be anything other than a founder, the chair, the CEO or the leader of the company is absolutely unthinkable. It is as if their entire reason for being might disintegrate if they had to do anything else. Identity is an addiction that's hard to give up when you are the current generation of any enterprise and there are no 12-step programs for shedding an identity addiction, no Identities

Anonymous. But with a system of emotional governance, the loss of an identity through transitioning a life role can be transformative.

For most of human history ritual was used to mark significant moments. Some rituals marked the cycles of time, such as the seasons and how human beings were meant to adjust to them. Others marked significant moments of transition in a person's life. In the modern West, outside of rituals associated with religions, it's more common to attach significant moments in our lives to privilege or material ownership—your first driver's license at 16 and the freedom to drive for example . Few of these loose rituals involve any emotional development.

Transition in life is not just an operational process; it's an emotional process. When the time comes to transition a business, an organization, or pass the torch in a family or a group it can feel like everything a leader has ever known, everything they have built their identity upon, is being torn away from them. It can feel like a kind of death. Leaders don't desire a lifelong vacation. They want to strive toward purpose. One day a founder or leader wakes up and they are no longer the one in charge. The responsibilities and the vision for the organization is now in someone else's hands. And overnight, they have been pushed to the side and replaced with a newer, younger version of themselves. Suddenly, their identity is gone. There is nothing. Adapting to this isn't simple or easy.

This uncharted emotional terrain could be a dark and confusing place for those accustomed to their hard-won perch atop the highest summit. No one wants to be back on the valley floor, looking up at a new even higher summit. It could feel like a failure, or it might feel so daunting and impossible to overcome. They could say to themselves, "I've already worked so hard, and sacrificed everything to accomplish what I have, and I am *tired*." Many leaders and visionaries have spent a life building only to find the destination is a closed door. The biggest challenge any individual has is in being aware of their impostor—the part that says, "I am the business." But the organization is something you built. Your identity is as a leader; that's something you do.

We think we are what we do and what we built as equivalent to who we are. That is the imposter.

Inside, we already know succession is necessary. We can't hold on to what we've built forever. To evolve and grow, the current generation in transitioning the vision to the next generation, will have to grieve the loss of their identity. They will need to dig deep within themselves to find the courage to begin their ascent to a new summit and toward a new life goal. This is the first reframing that is required.

Confronting your impostor—losing your default identity—will cause an upsurge of complex, even conflicting emotions that aren't much different from what someone in recovery from a lifetime of addiction might feel. In some cultures, especially in the West, we might have a difficult time naming these emotions for what they are: Grief. Grieving doesn't only come when you lose a loved one. People grieve over loss in general. It's normal. In fact, it's a vital tool for processing loss when you have the conversations that simply allow it to be.

The Māori people of New Zealand observe *tangihanga*, a communal mourning process that can span several days. When a loved-one dies, the deceased—along with their clothing and personal artifacts—is brought to a communal meeting place where the community gathers to pay their respects. They give speeches, sing songs, and share stories. The grief is expressed openly and communally. The event concludes with a farewell ceremony, followed by the cleansing of the deceased's home and a communal feast.

In Okinawa, people believe that a person's *mabui*—their spirit—can be displaced by the shock of sudden and significant life changes. The *Mabui-gumi* ritual takes a person in that condition through a series of processes, including returning to the place of loss, collecting symbolic items, praying and offering food to ancestors. This ceremony helps the affected restore a sense of themselves after a disruption of their identity.

Each of these cultures and others like them around the world, is utilizing something universally essential in their grief traditions. They ritualize the process and frame it—in a communal context through ceremony—as an initiatory experience of transformation. Grief is not an option; it is an initiatory part of the ritual of transition. So, why aren't we doing this in succession? How do we adapt our Western models of grief to the emotional reality of letting go of the impostor—who may have served us well for a period of life—and living truer to ourselves?

Swiss-American psychiatrist Elisabeth Kübler-Ross in her 1969 book *On Death and Dying*, outlines five-stages of grief that humans experience during loss—denial, anger, bargaining, depression, and acceptance. Over time her model has become almost universally applied to other forms of loss beyond death and dying, divorce, job loss and especially loss of identity. By the mid-1970s Kübler-Ross would add that how we experience the stages isn't necessarily linear and that people can often oscillate between stages or even experience them simultaneously. By the 1990s David Kessler, who had been a longtime collaborator with Kübler-Ross, would add that, beyond acceptance, people could even come to derive purpose from their loss.

Here is a way to apply the five stages of grief to what could be a model of letting go of the impostor in your life:

1. **Denial.** *Is this really happening? Am I dreaming? I always knew the day would come when roles in our family would shift, but is it really now? How did time go so fast?*

2. **Anger.** *No way—I can't step back. I won't. I'm still the one who holds this family together. You may be grown now, you may make your own choices, but I'm not letting go. Not yet.* (Meanwhile, life has already started moving on around you.)

3. **Bargaining.** *Everyone is adjusting to the new way of doing things! Can't I just stay close? Let me help. I can still play an important role. I know I can still give something of value if only you'd let me remain a central part of things.*

4. **Depression.** This stage can take two forms. The first is: *Why did I step back? I still had more to give. The second is: Did I do something wrong? Did I fail my family? Maybe I should have done things differently, been more present, loved more openly. Maybe then I wouldn't feel so left behind now.*

5. **Acceptance.** *I've done what I could. It's someone else's turn now.*

Beyond acceptance and somewhere between the new valley floor and the new summit, we can find purpose in the loss. It's important to allow yourself the room to grieve and have the courage to grieve communally. A new identity can be carved out of the old one, and it can create a new future. A change of identity is needed to attain the summit.

Once we claim our place on the summit, we then have to learn to maintain it. Life will throw new challenges at us and without this process of undergoing a deep dive into the constructs we create to avoid fear and pain; we can be swept off the mountain. We have to intentionally design how we get our needs met in healthy ways and maintain those constructs to stay on the summit.

Author Michael Singer writes in his book *The Untethered Soul: The Journey Beyond the Self* that we all experience pain and fear in our lives, and we create many constructs to deal with our pain and fear, and "you will never find yourself in what you've built to define yourself." By actively facing our grief at the loss of our default identity and by using a system of emotional governance to master our feelings and internal narratives around succession, we can understand our Land of Familiar and build awareness that will enable us to ascend to a new and different summit.

If we learn to first have these conversations with ourselves, then eventually the understandings that arise will begin to emerge in how we interact with others—our associates, friends and family. It's inevitable that many complex and even frightening emotions will arise, and we need to be prepared to talk about them with others as we arrive at the Base Camp below our new summit. A system of communicating about our emotions—especially our grief—will enable us to build a new identity of meaning, purpose, and connection.

Questions to ponder

1. What actions, if any, do you take regularly that you would call an addiction?

2. Are you prepared to let go? Use the Emotional Readiness Tool available below to find out where you may be an imposter.

CHAPTER 7

The Great White Elephant

We all have that *thing* that we don't want to talk about. We can pretend it's not there and that we have no awareness of it, but it follows us from situation to situation, whispering to us the uncomfortable truth that, sooner or later, we will be forced to acknowledge its existence and confront it directly. For some of us that wake-up call can come in the form of a major health crisis, or the destruction of a marriage or a family. For others it can come in the form of the silent patterns that operate in our lives finally becoming disastrously misaligned with our current needs. The longer we put off confronting an uncomfortable truth, the greater the likelihood that we guarantee it will grow so big that we can no longer afford to ignore it.

Once known as Siam, the Kingdom of Thailand has a tradition that extends back to the fourteenth century CE. Kings of the Ayutthaya Kingdom (1351–1767), an empire including much of Southeast Asia, would receive a gift of white elephants from their courtiers as signs of their legitimacy. The elephant was considered a sacred symbol in the Hindu-Buddhist tradition, and white elephants were the rarest form of the sacred animal. For a king to own one was considered a divine sanction to rule. For centuries, the kings of Thailand would retain the rare white elephants in palatial stables and treat them like royalty—giving them noble titles, assigning them royal caretakers, and even holding state rituals and ceremonies in their honor.

Trailokanat of Ayutthaya (r. 1448–1488) had many white elephants and he used them to project dominance over his many rivals in both the dangerous jungles of neighboring Laos and the wild, and unclaimed highlands of Northern Thailand. It was as recently as 1910 that King Rama V (r. 1868–1910) made his white elephants' state symbols of awe and influences, featuring them on State flags, royal seals, and coinage.

However, the ownership of these sacred giants could be as much a burden as a blessing. The rare white elephants are enormously expensive to maintain, and because they were considered sacred, they could not be used for labor or warfare.

Both a symbol of divine blessing and an economic burden, for one king to offer another king the gift of a white elephant could be seen as a subtle curse or even a political trap. If a Thai king wanted to punish a noble who had fallen out of favor, indirectly and shrewdly disgracing him, he might gift him a white elephant. The noble wouldn't dare refuse or sell the sacred animal, and his courtiers expected him to lavishly care for it as tradition and religious custom demanded. The immense cost would inevitably ruin him financially and potentially destroy his position and legacy in the court. The idiom of the white elephant has made its way into Western culture to mean something that is more trouble than it's worth.

The white elephant is the thing that is costing you far too much not to address. For many of us the greatest uncomfortable truth we will face is the impostor—the identity we construct for ourselves that keeps us from facing reality.

In most areas of life we tend to focus on the *what* and the *how*, but not the *why*. What are the *feelings* of everyone involved? That is usually the white elephant in the room. Feelings can have a radioactive effect on people, relationships and systems. Acute exposure to the radiation of un-governed feelings is the substance of the conversations that are not being had. This could be about dad's rage, mom's alcoholism, or the favorite child who isn't applying themselves. It's something that's holding the family or the organization back from great things. The biggest risk we face is in remaining the impostor. Just as we have to identify and acknowledge our own impostor, our family and others involved in our lives could have their own impostors. It might show up in the behaviors that are not being talked about because we don't feel emotionally safe to have a conversation about them. The white elephant in the room is right there in front of us. First, we have to identify it. Then, we have to talk about it.

We're Not Taught How to Have Conversations

Picture this: A visionary has spent their life building something, and an identity around it. It's their pride, their legacy. Over the years, it gained a reputation: maybe it serves a noble mission, supports the community, or reflects deeply held values. Maybe they established a town museum or started a small business providing a vital service. Whatever it is it has symbolic prestige, even emotional sacredness within the family. Then, they pass it on to their child. Their creation is positioned as a gift, an honor.

What if, beneath the symbolism, lies an unspoken and hazardous reality? Their creation is outdated or debt-ridden. It consumes vast amounts of time and energy. The systems are a mess; the team reveres the founder—not any successor. The founder may still be alive and hovering, offering unsolicited advice or critique. The community sees the organization as "noble" or "essential." The family sees it as "a dream come true." But the successor sees it for what it is: something they thought they wanted, but in reality it is a slow drain on their freedom, finances, and mental health. They can't use it freely, can't remake it without backlash, and can't walk away without shame. To the next generation, the legacy they've inherited is a hallowed obligation wrapped in a heavy chain.

Worse, there could be emotional manipulation layered in: The next generation has a duty. Like the white elephant of Thai legend, the next generation inheriting the organization and both its value and liabilities cannot say no without being seen as ungrateful or disrespectful. The organization is now a mirror: reflecting the values of the giver, the guilt of the receiver, and the tension between past practices and today's needs.

A Roman statesman and philosopher from the first century BCE., Marcus Tullius Cicero, said, "If we are not ashamed to think it, we should not be ashamed to say it." Cicero lived during a time of deep political instability and upheaval in the late Roman Empire, marked by coups d'état, civil war, and political violence and chaos in the Roman streets. Even as the world around him fell apart, Cicero avidly believed the Roman institutions of debate, oration and the power of ideas were the only true way to solve Rome's seemingly insurmountable problems. Ultimately, he inspired millions who came after him—including the framers of the United States Constitution. Quintilian, a Roman scholar and teacher who came into prominence years after Cicero's death later said about his idol, "Cicero was not the name of a man, but of eloquence itself." So, communication is important. But what kind of communication? Not all of us have the silver tongue of Cicero. The good news is that communication is a muscle; it can be strengthened.

Healthy relational dynamics between people start with communicating about the underlying feelings such as anger, shame, grief, mistrust, or control. Your past conditioning could be the Great White Elephant in the room, holding you back and causing havoc inside the family, group or organization. No matter how intelligent we are, emotions will trump that intelligence. No school in the world teaches us how to have these conversations, or how to ask the right questions to navigate the complex nuances of human emotions. The focus in our institutions is always on the tangible parts, never on the intangibles.

Unveiling the Issues

The first idea to understand is that all of us feel entitled to our emotional traditions and beliefs. Sometimes, feelings we feel entitled to are collectively our white elephant. We avoid facing it or talking about it because it is *ours.* It is part of us, and we will fight to keep it in the center of the room.

One of the biggest examples of this is the ideas we have around money and ideas that are shaped by our family's emotional traditions around money.

One common emotional tradition around money is that making too much is shameful and we should feel guilt around it.

Another common emotional tradition around money, one that often occurs when young people inherit money, is what I (and most of the world) would call *the entitled brat.*

At first glance, you might think the entitled brat is what it sounds like—a child throwing a tantrum at the grocery store; a child of rich parents playing out the trust-fund stereotype. In my book, *Entitled Brat or Contributing Leader?* I examined this phenomenon, and I realized every human being on Earth feels entitled to their thoughts, beliefs, judgments and prejudices, and ultimately our emotional traditions. Not just celebrities, not just children of billionaires, but every one of us.

The truth is, we all have the entitled brat inside of us in this way. We all feel entitled to the external world responding to our feelings in whatever way we prefer. This trait is inherent in humans because, as babies before we have language, we are entirely dependent on our caregivers in order to survive. If we don't find a way to communicate our needs through our feelings—crying or throwing a tantrum—we don't get our needs met and we don't survive. It can take years of social conditioning for us to grow out of this.

I once worked with a client on a strategy to transfer some of his business wealth to his children. One of his daughters spent impulsively instead of saving and investing any of it. As we dug deeper in conversations about why this was happening, it came out that her belief was, "Money can't keep me emotionally safe, and it only brings trouble." Unnerved and threatened by the money, she would push it away.

Another daughter of wealth, Janice, told me that, as her parents started to make money and gain affluent friends, their social circle grew chaotic. It was soon full of divorce, drug abuse, and a lifestyle full of dopamine chasing. She decided she didn't want money because of what it led to. Janice longed for the "simple" times where her family would go on holidays with the camper van, laugh, and have time together as a family.

Janice's father's story is a classic immigrant tale of pursuing the American Dream. He built financial wealth for his family in his new home country—something his own father had been unable to do in war torn Europe after World War II.

Today Janice is very involved in the business and chairs the family foundation. And she can talk and think about money in a healthy way because she was able to identify the money imposter in her.

Emotional traditions that form around resources—whether material resources like money, or the intangible emotional resources—don't just form in highly-resourced families. In every part of the world, how we manage money is related to how we manage relationships. Regardless of whether we grow up with a lot of money, or very little, we might end up with the same problem. We might believe that money is dangerous, or in contrast, a tool for good. To identify one of the primary drivers of the patterns in our lives, we need to understand our beliefs about money.

I met Henry when he was a sensitive, ambitious man in his 40s. In the early 1960s, when Henry was eight, his parents left Hong Kong for Canada. They carried two battered suitcases and a great deal of unspoken fear about what their future in the West might have in store for them. His father had once run a small and esteemed printing shop in Kowloon, but in Vancouver he found himself washing dishes in the back of a Chinese take-out restaurant. His mother, a seamstress, altered dresses in a rented flat above a convenience store.

Money was always tight. The sound of coins clinking in glass jars was the soundtrack to Henry's childhood. Rent reminders pushed through the letterbox were a constant reminder of how precarious their situation was, while his parents' whispered arguments in the kitchen when they thought he was asleep. At school, he wore second-hand Reeboks and kept his head down when classmates showed off brand-name trainers or talked about summer holidays abroad.

Though he was clever, Henry's earliest lessons were in feeling small. Poverty clung to him like an invisible stain. He avoided asking for anything. He avoided drawing attention, convinced that wanting anything from anyone would only highlight what his family lacked. Over time, that pervasive feeling of lack became a simmering feeling of shame: Henry measured himself against others through what he could not afford, through all the spaces where his family's absence of wealth made him feel like he did not belong.

Henry's father was grappling with his own shame. In Kowloon he had been a respected member of the community who provided an important service, although it only enabled his family to live modestly. In order to start his printing shop, he needed to borrow a large sum of money from his cousin who had ties to organized crime. For Henry's father, the borrowed money came with a substantial shame attached to it. He felt that, in taking the loan, he was taking the easy way out of honest hardship and he wanted Henry to do anything but repeat his mistake. He would tell Henry that the only thing he could do that ever mattered was go to business school and become a legitimate businessman. Henry would not be allowed to have friends. He would not be allowed to play sports or join after school clubs. His father insisted that Henry speak only English and never use his native Cantonese. For Henry's father, his shame created a family environment of strict control.

Like Henry, you might come from a tradition of control, and part of that tradition is that your family minimizes your successes. They believe that, to make you strong and upright, you will need to be raised in a tough-love environment. Instead of looking at your inevitable missteps as a way to learn, gain confidence and grow in the world, they call out your failures and shame you for them. Perhaps for decades, you internalize these habits, and they become unhealthy, dysfunctional traditions that are ritualized through your behavior.

Eventually, you build a life for yourself; you've created its vision, processes and identity and you've watched yourself thrive. Now *you're* in control. But when the time comes to transition the business over to the next generation of leadership, you dig in your heels and resist. You feel entitled to be in control of what you built, and you have a difficult time *emotionally* letting go, because part of what you feel entitled to has become part of your identity—your impostor.

Maybe instead, you come from a family where any display of uncomfortable or inconvenient emotion was met with disapproval or dismissal. If you were upset and your parent or guardian felt their own anger or frustration with your feelings, they might say something like, "I don't like you right now."

We don't know how to process this as children and so we internalize it to mean that we are bad and wrong. We feel it means *I don't like you and stop expressing yourself like that.* We shut down. We interpret their anger as a signal that we should never open up and express our feelings. Years of suppressing our own feelings, believing that emotions are not okay, turns into repression and maybe even addiction; drugs, alcohol, toxic relationships, or other destructive behaviors. We might then have a difficult time breaking through to a healthier degree of connection with others because of our own self-rejection.

Moving away from these corrosive uncertainties and destructive behaviors means moving to base camp. In our model of the ascent, base camp is a communal place. Here is where you connect with other climbers and share your experiences, skills and understandings of the mountain's terrain—where you acknowledge and communicate the feelings that are showing up. Base camp is where you prepare to ascend the mountain. Every climber arriving at base camp arrives with two key tools already with them: A manifesto and a checklist.

The **manifesto** is the first part of claiming who you will be when you reach the summit. It is a set of positive affirmations that you create. Affirmations that transform the patterns that meet your six human needs from meeting them in unhealthy ways to meeting them in healthy ways. It is created through internally mapping the feelings, emotional traditions, and your stories about both that you are bringing to the mountain.

For example: My manifesto is, "beautiful and precious." I faced the impostor that had kept me in my Land of Familiar, the one that had said, "you are dirty, ugly, unloved, and it's all your fault," and decided that was no longer going to be the story I told myself about myself. I created a new story about myself by mapping my Land of Familiar—a concept we're about to explore in depth—and re-orienting myself around a new set of beliefs.

Questions to Help You Create a Manifesto

1. When you're in a low, uncertain, or overwhelmed place, what emotions are present?

2. When facing difficulty and uncertainty, what habits, people, or thoughts help you gain perspective?

3. What does your emotional low reveal about unmet needs, buried truths, or priorities in your life?

4. How do you respond to any recurring moods, stressors, or thought loops that show up like unwelcome weather patterns?

5. Who are the people who help you through stressful times and are also there to celebrate the good times?

The **Checklist** is a list of tools and strategies to use around the kind of conversations and communication you will need to be able to have while at base camp. The kind of listening you will need to do. The skills to hold on to yourself and govern your feelings and defensive reactions when others are expressing feelings or perceptions you might find uncomfortable. There are four goals for communication as you prepare for the ascent:

- **Build trust,**
- **Synchronize intention**,
- **Clarify roles, and**
- **Cultivate the psychological resilience needed for what lies ahead.**

To complete these goals, you first need to establish six types of communication with the other climbers at base camp.

Six Types of Communication at Base Camp

1. **Clarity Communication: "Why are we making this ascent?"**
    - » What am I hoping to gain from this ascent—externally and internally?
    - » What vision are we aligning with as a relational unit?
    - » Where are we headed, and what does success feel like?

By examining clarity communication, we are orienting the compass before the ascent and anchoring our shared purpose and personal meaning for the effort ahead.

2. **Honesty Communication: "What are my limits right now?"**
    - » What hazards am I afraid of on my ascent?
    - » Where am I under-resourced or emotionally fatigued?
    - » What support needs do I need to communicate before we begin?

To practice truthful, compassionate disclosures of capacity, fear, and need we need to understand our perceptions of the emotional terrain that lies ahead of us and the stories we are telling ourselves about the perceived emotional hazards of the ascent.

3. **Boundaries & Agreements Communication: "How will we move together?"**
    - » What pace is sustainable?
    - » How will we make decisions mid-ascent?
    - » What are our roles—and how do we coordinate them?
    - » How will we handle missteps or disagreements?

Using these questions, both internally and with others, we can clarify relational expectations and coordinate the ascent—this is like double-checking the ropes before attempting the face.

4. **Contingency Communication: "What if something goes wrong?"**
    - How do we want to respond if someone struggles or gets stuck in a difficult emotion?
    - What's our emergency signal—how do we pause and regroup?
    - What will help us feel safe admitting we're overwhelmed?

To prepare psychologically and practically for adversity, this is the communication equivalent of packing your survival gear.

5. **Appreciative Communication: "What strengths are we bringing?"**
    - What do I admire or trust in those (family, friends, and/or associates) who are along with me in this emotional ascent?
    - What unique skill or mindset do I bring to this ascent?
    - What unique skill or mindset do others bring to this ascent?

To build morale, mutual respect, and trust, mutual acknowledgement builds confidence in each person's role in ascent.

6. **Ritual or Intentional Communication: "How do we mark the beginning?"**
    - Is there a phrase, gesture, or shared intention we want to offer before we begin?
    - How do we mark each milestone of the ascent?
    - Can we create a way of grounding that connects us back to this base when things get hard?

This is a ceremonial fire before the climb—it centers us and those supporting us before we set out on the ascent. We might use symbolic language, or ceremony that marks intention, highlights meaning, and aligns intention.

Once you leave base camp, leave the Great White Elephant behind. You cannot afford to carry that kind of heavy load to the summit.

Questions to ponder:

1. What could you be holding onto in your life that is taking up resources that will affect your ascent—emotional or otherwise?

2. What kind of culture do you want to create at base camp?

3. What would it feel like to arrive at base camp and feel truly heard, resourced, and prepared?

4. What's one communication habit you could bring into your base-camp moments (group meetings, life planning, emotional resets)?

CHAPTER 8

The Anatomy of Walls

Throughout history, walls have been defensive structures, meant to keep out the world's threats; predators, rival tribes, enemy armies, disease, even others we label undesirable in some way—justified or unjustified. They exist to protect what we care about, what we have defined as vulnerable, our resources, our families, heads of state, or religious and cultural icons.

The earliest walls were probably like the *boma* in India—thorny brambles of acacia branches, cut and stacked to keep predators out of human camps. Then walls became simple wooden palisades with a single entrance. Over time, as human societies became more complex, and more importantly, interconnected—through trade and diplomacy—the walls became more intricate: more gates, more obstacles, defensive features such as earthworks, drawbridges, moats, towers, barbicans and portcullises. More controls dictated who could enter and who could leave our walls.

By the late Middle Ages in Europe, having impervious and opulent walls was as much a symbol of a king's status and authority as it was a structure to protect what was precious. But walls offer us two dangerous illusions: **the illusion of safety and the illusion of control**. They can be costly to maintain, require regular maintenance, and restrict growth. Inevitably, the city they are meant to protect will outgrow them and as people move to the uncluttered and abundant land beyond the walls, new walls will have to be built; the cycle continues.

On May 29, 1452, the great city of Constantinople—a sprawling, and opulent ancient metropolis clinging to the Bosporus strait in what is now modern-day Turkey—was assaulted and sacked by the Ottoman Empire. Once the seat of the Eastern Roman Empire, Constantinople (now Istanbul) had stood since its founding in 330 CE under Christian Roman Emperor Constantine the Great. For eleven centuries the city had been besieged many times, but its walls withstood the attacks.

Constructed in the fifth century CE. by Roman Emperor Theodosius II, and built of straight-cut limestone, these walls had stood for 800 years and were considered by many to be the finest example of defensive structures in existence at that time. The Ottomans army had laid siege to Constantinople for a span of two full months. The thick aroma of wood fires and siege would have hung heavy in the air—spices, incense, the bitter tang of rain, the sweet and acrid mix of the dead. Carried on the black smoke that rose into the air above the rolling plains that straddled the Lycus River, sounded the Muslim call to prayer, like a song , haunting and beautiful.

For 54 days the Ottomans ebbed and surged like a sea of steel, sweat and blood, 50,000 men-at-arms threw themselves against the great walls of Theodoricus in colossal waves. On the walls the Byzantine archers would have nervously knocked their arrows, drew crossbow bolts tight, and prayed.

Enter Orban, a Hungarian engineer who offered the Ottoman Sultan Mehmed II a great bombardment which he swore to the sultan could, "blast the walls of Babylon itself." Orban's "royal gun" was an 8.2-meter (27-foot) long monster capable of hurling a 600-pound cannonball over 1.6 km (1 mile). It took three hours to reload, but loosing a hail of iron and fire against the walls a barrage crashed into the thick stone. And another. And another. The Ottoman guns were able to bring down the great Theodosian walls in a day. The walls that had kept out invaders since 1204 were forever breached and the Ottomans poured into the city.

The walled city is the psyche's last stand—fortified, guarded, and watchful. Just as humans build physical walls as protection from external threats or as a form of mastery over a dangerous and unpredictable external environment, we also build internal walls that are meant to protect our emotions. We think these psychological walls will protect our inner world from being invaded, hurt, or overwhelmed.

As the story of the fall of Constantinople shows us, in a siege, the attacker waits. They cut off resources, supplies, communication, and the morale of the defenders is slowly consumed by attrition. Internal decay, disease, rebellion, madness, and starvation become the daily reality of those defended by the walls.

The enemy outside can be less destructive than the isolation within.

Even if they are meant to defend us, psychological walls don't just keep threats out—they also cut off nourishment: love, connection, intimacy, and meaning. Futility and the threat of inevitable harm feels inevitable and overwhelming. Over time, the "defended" person starves emotionally, socially, and spiritually. Prolonged emotional fortification could lead to Operator Syndrome, emotional numbness, or identity confusion. We forget who we are without the wall.

What Begins as a Defense Ends as a Prison

Psychological walls eventually fail—through breakdowns, flashbacks, uncontrollable emotions, or failed relationships. And like breached cities, the results can be catastrophic if there has been no preparation for contact, trust, or interdependence. **Either we open the gates with intention, or they will be forced open in crisis.** The results can be catastrophic.

Walls Keep Out Allies, Too

In a siege, even help cannot enter without risk. Psychological walls do not discriminate. They block threats and support alike. Genuine love, healing, or connection must batter the gates or be turned away. In defending against all pain, you also bar love. When you create a wall to keep out frustration or pain you also end up keeping out the good.

Walls are deceptive. They can lull us into the complacency brought on by a false sense of security and they can be overcome by outside forces that eventually innovate beyond our ability to adapt. Walls give the illusion of strength by keeping the threat outside. All the while, they can also hide what is weakening inside. So, why do we continue to build them?

Withdrawal behind a wall is not a permanent destination—**you can't stay there if you value emotional, psychological and physical freedom**.

Questions to ponder:

1. What walls have you built in your life?

2. What do you think your walls are protecting you from?

3. What is the good that might be kept out by your walls?

4. How would the wall need to change to become a gateway instead of a barrier?

5. What kind of relationship would make you feel safe enough to open a door in the wall?

CHAPTER 9

The Theater of Family

Our past shapes our present. Without an internal guidance system, we humans tend to replicate whatever we have experienced in life and whatever has been modeled for us by our parents and guardians or what other influential people have taught us. Consider this: Why do so many of us stay in abusive relationships? Why do so many drugs or alcohol abusers relapse within thirty days of leaving rehab? Why are so many of us attracted to emotionally unavailable partners? Or emotionally tumultuous ones?

Anyone who has driven a car knows that there are places you drive every day that become so familiar to you over time—and through repetition—that you are eventually driving them on muscle memory. Any change in the routine pattern of our commute, or our Saturday circuit for errands, can be especially disruptive. We might become agitated, irritable, or anxious at road works, traffic, an obstacle in the road or an accident.

Our nervous system is driving the car, and it expects the familiar, a predictable set of conditions. Anything that breaks the pattern is a potential threat—it's incapable of caring whether those conditions are actually healthy for us or not.

Throughout our lives, we often stay in the familiar because leaving what's familiar can be frightening. We might fear that, to leave what has become our normal, we will lose our identity, lose our purpose, lose our edge. We could fear that a new familiar will be treacherous, possibly even deadly, to navigate. We might even feel that we deserve what we've grown accustomed to in the familiar, even if it's a perilous landscape filled with shame, dysfunctional relationships and worse memories.

For John du Pont, the financial wealth and opulence he grew up with at Foxcatcher Farm created distance and isolated him from secure connection with others. His normal was extreme emotional deprivation. Dave Schultz was one of the few people close enough to du Pont to try and help him regulate his volatile swings of emotion. Schultz ultimately became the target of du Pont's paranoia and violent psychotic break—possibly because Schultz was the one person close enough to do Pont to matter.

For me, my familiar was chaos. I knew that when my dad was away, I'd be sexually abused by my mother. When my dad came home, I knew I was getting a beating. It was highly dysfunctional and destructive, but to us, it was our normal.

As I started to do this counseling work, I would experience glimpses of peace and ease—the opposite of the chaos that had been my normal for so long. A part of me hadn't yet begun to trust situations that didn't feel chaotic and inside I would say to myself, "this doesn't feel normal!" So, I would revert back to the chaos that I was used to.

The truth is, leaving your old familiar and migrating across unknown and perilous terrain will be risky. But there is a map, in fact you already carry a piece of that map inside of you. Just like a sailor can read the stars, or a climber can read the rock face, we can read the emotional terrain of the land of the familiar we have called home—its winds, its patterns, its traits. We can recognize them in new terrain, and we can thrive.

The Land of Familiar

The emotional environment we grow used to in our lives is a terrain called The Land of Familiar. It is a way of conceptualizing how the patterns we inherit become normal to our nervous systems and continuously shape our lives. You can think of The Land of Familiar as an inverted pyramid, buried deep in the ground. At the narrowest point of the pyramid is a young child, crying for mama. The baby is hungry, but doesn't get fed by mama, so the child thinks in some raw fashion, "Hmm, Mom doesn't love me."

That first thought flows up the pyramid to the second section. Here, the child is forced to go to a school they don't want to attend. Some of the kids are mean, excluding them or bullying. They feel isolated and dissociate from learning, thinking, "My parents make me go to his horrible place. They don't protect me."

The third section, a little higher up the pyramid, occurs years later. Now a little older, the child finds attraction in another but doesn't have that feeling reciprocated. The child is rejected from job applications. They are denied experiences others are having, concluding "I'm not good enough. I'm a reject. I'm unlovable. I'm unwanted." Life experiences trickle to the point of the pyramid, buried deep in the ground; the smallest and most vulnerable part that all the other layers and their meanings are heaped on top of. There is the foundation: The memories and feelings that make up that child's Land of Familiar.

Your Land of Familiar is easy to spot. It shows up in your actions, behaviors, in the way you approach everyday situations and in the stories you tell yourself about both. These stories become emotional traditions that become patterns; we break the patterns, or the patterns break us. Why is this pattern breaking so hard? If you go back twelve generations before you and me, how many of your ancestors were involved in creating you? Let's round it off to 4094. That is how many of your ancestors lived and died and fought and married and loved and had children and struggled to pass down their genes to you. When it comes to confronting and changing the patterns that might be running your life, that is how much resistance you are up against.

Consider the people you know in your own life. If you know them well enough you might see the patterns that play out in their lives. They might tell you over-and-over-again about a new risky business opportunity that will be a success unlike the last time, or a new relationship and how *this* time it's going to work out. You might feel a pang of apprehension hearing about yet another orbit of a long-established pattern, knowing that the pattern that has played out before will likely continue. Examples of familiar patterns that play out in families include lack of emotional connection, harsh judgment, humor as deflection, sense of duty to family dynamics, and many, many more.

It may seem frightening that every human being on Earth can be so easily affected by the environmental conditions that existed before we were even born; it may feel like we are all fated to live out a set of patterns that we didn't choose. From a physiological perspective, how does this mechanism work?

What's Past is Prologue

Researchers in epigenetics suggest that external factors and conditions affect gene expression in the human body. Environmental factors such as trauma can imprint on an organism through epigenetic markers that turn "on" or turn "off" genes. If reproduced through offspring, that change leaves a biological imprint on a person's descendants—even without exposure to the original trauma, circumstance, or event.

In 1944, one of the harshest winters in a century gripped wartime Europe. In the Nazi-occupied Netherlands, a railroad strike had crippled Hitler's war machine, preventing men and munitions from reaching the German Wehrmacht's defense against Operation Market Garden—the Allied operation to liberate the Netherlands. In response to the Dutch strikes, the German Kriegsmarine—Hitler's nearly unstoppable navy—blockaded the Western Netherlands. By winter the Dutch canals, vital arteries for transporting food and supplies to the embattled Dutch people had hardened into thick ice. Over 20,000 people died of starvation while many suffered lifelong trauma and other health effects.

In 2008 researchers studying the Dutch population found that individuals prenatally exposed to famine during the Dutch Hunger Winter had less DNA methylation—a biological process that influences gene expression without altering DNA—compared to their unexposed, same-sex siblings. These findings shocked the scientific community, demonstrating that individuals with in-utero famine exposure showed an accelerated pace of biological aging six decades later, as measured by epigenetic clocks, even though they hadn't technically been born when the famine occurred.

Further studies have offered intriguing insights into the epigenetics of intergenerational trauma. A 2015 study published in *Biological Psychiatry* involved 32 Holocaust survivors and 22 adult children of these same survivors. Differences surfaced in the way a gene that regulates cortisol functioned. Cortisol helps the body manage stress so lower performance translates into a diminished ability to do that. Many survivors and their children were affected. Control group studies in eight Jewish parent-child pairs with no direct ties to the Holocaust did not show this difference.

If these cycles and emotional patterns are created before we are born, how do we reverse the change? Science tells us that some changes can be reversed through therapeutic intervention, and others can be partially reversed. "Therapeutic intervention" can be as simple as shifts toward healthier eating and relationships to complicated chemical interventions. The good news for many people is that those healthy shifts offer a lot of hope in leaving an epigenetic white elephant behind.

Organizations in the Land of Familiar

If we scale the Land of Familiar up one more time, from the individual to the family and finally to the organization, we see how the same patterns and cycles play out over generations of an organization. Just like people, any human enterprise has its own normalized patterns that operate

When groups face a systemic internal problem, managers deploy a process or standard implementation to resolve it. It is a reasonable response, but if the nature of the problem is an emotional one, arising out of patterns and narratives at the individual level, or at the level of the organization's emotional culture, it won't work. Documenting a process on some piece of paper that hangs inside the break room isn't going to change someone's Land of Familiar. It can't recreate a person's past and change their behaviors. Only acknowledging a person's past can do that. Going back to the drawing board, bringing up these memories, and having a process to discuss them can possibly create the conditions that, over time and with enough repetition, can change a person's epigenetics. Nothing within a person will change until they have a new Land of Familiar. Until they become comfortable enough with themselves and those within their family to talk about the white elephant in the room.

What's your family's white elephant?

Visionaries in the Land of Familiar

Visionaries who create organizations typically carry the emotional imprint of origin and survival. They often see the business as a personal extension—like the child they might have raised through hardship, improvisation, and intense devotion. Even after stepping down, founders may unconsciously seek affirmation or control, acting out patterns of parental attachment, fear of irrelevance, or resentment when their legacy feels altered. Their emotional narrative often includes pride, anxiety over dilution of original values, and a resistance to perceived unnecessary change. This can create a subtle gravitational pull in the organization, where the founder's presence—either literal or symbolic—shapes the emotional climate and decision-making long after formal authority has shifted.

Parents in the Land of Familiar

Parents occupy a tension-filled middle-ground; caught between honoring the family legacy and raising the next generation. Emotional patterns in this group could include guilt for deviating from the founder's ways, anxiety about performance and loyalty, and unconscious resistance to mentoring the next generation due to fears of being displaced. They may also over-identify with the family's emotional legacy swinging between preservation and innovation in a way that reflects unresolved inner conflict about authority, tradition, and their role or place in the family's life cycle.

The Next Generation in the Land of Familiar

Children growing into adulthood, or any successor growing into greater autonomy might grapple with a nagging anxiety: unconscious patterns of individuation, approval-seeking, and imposter syndrome are only a few of the challenges they might be facing. They could feel pressure to both differentiate from previous leadership and to prove themselves worthy of the inheritance, leading to internalized conflicts around risk-taking and self-expression. Some often unconsciously enact the role of the eldest child in a family system—tasked with carrying responsibility without full autonomy. Others may unconsciously rebel—introducing bold changes to assert independence—while others over-conform, mimicking past behaviors out of fear of rejection or failure. For some, the guilt of being "born lucky" could be their white elephant.

In planning any succession, your job is to leave what you built in capable hands. The first step is to think of what you built as something that will outlast you. This can be tougher to do for the visionary founder than any other succeeding generation. Creating something that will outlive you is quite an accomplishment, but it can be tough to let go of. Some visionaries fight with everything they have to keep it in their hands. But that's not what makes a great organization or a great family. There is no legacy there. Someone with this mindset isn't focusing on the long game, just the short one.

Longevity means endurance through constant evolution. **A family's emotional legacy that is viewed as lasting through generations will be managed differently than one focused on short-term goals.** Life is dynamic. Events and circumstances will arise, threatening to drag you back into your Land of Familiar. A new white elephant will take up residence in the room. If we bottle-up the emotions that come with these situations, we will change for the worse. If we allow our emotions to control us, they will get the best of us. Often when I talk about installing a system in a business to govern emotions I hear, "I simply don't have the time, Franco. I can't take on another task. And neither can my family. We have a business to run."

Without a system of emotional governance and a process for managing these emotions, we risk damage to the business and the family.

Creating a Safe Space for the emotions to be put on the table and discussed communally is how we create a system of emotional governance. A Safe Space is probably what you didn't get enough of as a child and still seek out as an adult. It is a set of agreements that allows frank conversation with yourself and another person without fear of judgement; a way of saying, *what I have shared is important to me*, and asking, *is that safe with you?*

To understand your Land of Familiar, you need emotional awareness. *Then* you must communicate that emotional awareness to others. As those conversations take place on e thing will become crystal clear: We are all immigrants in the Land of Familiar.

Questions to ponder:

1. What emotional dynamics from your early life (family, school, or culture) feel most familiar in your relationships or life decisions today?

2. When you're under pressure, which emotional role do you tend to fall into—rescuer, rebel, caretaker, outsider, controller—and who taught you to play that part?

3. What unspoken emotional "contracts" have you inherited or made with others in your life (for example "I'll never do as well as them," "I must prove I belong," "Success means loyalty to the past")?

4. What kinds of people or situations at work evoke unusually strong emotional reactions in you, and what do those reactions remind you of from your personal history?

5. In what ways might emotional familiarity be keeping you in a loop of predictability rather than allowing for genuine innovation, intimacy, or transformation?

CHAPTER 10

The Empty Space

What is a Safe Space?

Some of you may have felt a pang of discomfort in encountering those words and that's okay. The sad fact is that safe spaces in today's world of mass media influencers and the global living room of the internet are often places where all of us are enabled to use our feelings of victimization to disempower others. We might publicly use our feelings to shame or punish others for acting in ways that we perceive as transgressive. We might make them perform contrition and promise never to do something again so that we can feel better. These kinds of safe spaces put the emphasis in the wrong place—What is "out there" versus what's on the inside, where we have the ability to design our own future.

Why do we need a Safe Space? As I explored in my book *Safe Space: Governance in Action*, we all want to feel safe, in ourselves, in our relationships with others—especially our families. That sense of safety extends to our broader social groups, such as the community or the nation. A feeling of safety is the prerequisite for getting anything done when in cooperation with others. Our decisions, our ability to lead and to be led. Safety isn't just an abstract feeling, it's something we can create through a deliberate process of conversation, about feelings, about conflicts and challenges. To solve problems, we have to reach a consensus—a Latin word borrowed from *com* meaning "with, together" and *sentire* meaning "to feel." So, a consensus is to feel together. In modern usage, a consensus is a general agreement; a group solidarity in sentiment and belief around the nature of something, and in the realms of politics and administration an agreement around a course of action to be undertaken. A deliberate process of conversation gets everyone on the same page so that we can reach a consensus—feeling together.

In 411 BCE, the civil foundations that had once held mighty Athens together for hundreds of years were forcefully shaken by one of its greatest rivals: the city of Syracuse in Sicily. A military expedition to distant Sicily had recently ended in catastrophe; an entire fleet of 200 ships had been burned or captured and thousands of *Hoplites*—the most disciplined and trained Greek soldiers, who fought in tight formation with great spears—were either enslaved or dead.

In response to such a colossal defeat, Athens was on the brink of financial ruin. The nearby villages scattered throughout the rocky, arid Greek countryside that depended on Athens for stability and defense, began to break away from Athenian influence, descending into a boiling of civil unrest. A faction of wealthy and influential Athenians, many of whom were disillusioned with the ability of their democratic Assembly to manage the war, conspired to overthrow the Assembly. Theramenes—a persuasive Athenian statesmen, prominent general and one of the leaders of this idealist faction—sprang into quick and decisive action.

Within days of the defeat, Theramenes staged a coup d'état, overthrowing the democratic government of Athens in a bloodless seizure of power and installing a carefully selected council of 400 Athenian oligarchs to rule the rapidly crumbling city state. Theramenes and his supporters argued that a smaller, elite ruling body could better negotiate peace with Athens' enemies and restore stability to the state.

The Athenians had, for hundreds of years, maintained The Agora, a central public square used as a space for public discourse, debate and administration of issues involving the Athenian people. Here, legal disputes could be argued publicly, and personal grievances could be brought before juries or magistrates. Though it excluded women, slaves, and non-citizens, The Agora *logos*—dialogue and persuasion—were highly valued and a cornerstone of a democratic society.

Across to the West from where the Acropolis stands in Athens and towering above The Agora, is The Pnyx—a hill with a great stone seating area and the stone steps of a platform for orators carved into its bleached stone cliffs. The nearly mythic hero Peracles had once stood there, leading Athens to glory during its golden age as did Demosthenes, one of the greatest orators in Western history. The Pnyx had been the gathering place for the Athenian Assembly—The primary legislative body for the city state. Here 6,000 male citizens could gather to debate matters of economy, law, war, and foreign policy. Attendees on The Pnyx practiced *isegoria*—the equal right of any citizen, not just the elites, to address the Assembly.

During the rule of the 400 oligarchs installed by Theramenes's coup, a few ardent democratic sympathizers continued to meet clandestinely. There at The Pnyx members of the Athenian navy, who were democratic loyalists, and the poorest citizens of Athens, who had the most to lose from the coup, discussed their grievances openly and resolved to bring down Theramenes's 400 usurpers.

As fear of civil war spread throughout these public spaces and beyond the boundaries of Athens, the 400 grew increasingly paranoid and they began to turn on each other. After a mere four months of chaotic misrule, the 400 themselves were overthrown and the citizens of Athens began to restore their democracy. Today the orator's steps on The Pnyx still stand and are considered around the world to be the birthplace of democracy.

The ancient Athenians were able to resolve their political and military crisis of 411 BC because they maintained a Safe Space: A dialogue-driven place where the people could express their concerns and feelings about the oligarchic government that had seized power. The Athenians made preserving this social institution of their Safe Space necessary and essential to how their society functioned.

Societies and groups that have ignored or suppressed models of deliberative governance aren't hard to find in history, and the consequences have been usually disastrous. Happening against the backdrop of the Soviet Union's collapse, the unstitching of Yugoslavia—a multi-ethnic federation in Eastern Europe—from 1990 to 1992, was a harrowing drama of brutal warfare, ethnic violence and ideological suppression. The Soviet Union was not an environment that allowed for a Safe Space to engender transition and collaboration.

In family and in life at large the battlefield is what is often created when the familiar patterns of the family and the familiar patterns of individuals collide. For many visionaries, by the time the organization has been built and is thriving, they could already be on the battlefield—or very near to it.

Some families see the conflict and think it's their normal. Other families don't see the conflict, while even others know there's conflict, because they can feel it simmering in their interactions, but they don't understand why.

How do we reclaim a safe space and put it to work for the family in a healthy way?

Base Camp and the Safe Space

A Safe Space is the thing we've been longing for that we believe we'll get from the outside, but we can give it to ourselves by understanding what's on the inside. The first thing to understand is that, when it comes to our feelings, the things we are trying to get for ourselves externally by controlling, manipulating, convincing, bargaining, or influencing others are the first things that we have to find a way to give to ourselves. If, for example, we need acceptance and validation, we need to recognize that we could be in an inherited familiar pattern. That need might be driving us to meet it in unhealthy ways such as trying to extract it from others.

Revisiting Maslow's hierarchy of needs, self-actualization is supported by the other needs of physiological, safety, love and belonging, and esteem. They are the foundation, base and structure of the pyramid and without them, self-actualization might be harder to reach. The distractions of basic needs can easily pull a person's attention away from lofty goals. Self-actualization is also where Maslow placed creativity and the need to solve problems. When we aren't consumed with meeting survival needs, in general, we can shift more of our attention and energy to co-creating.

Just because you might feel a need to get something from someone else doesn't mean that you're dysfunctional. It's natural for humans to be somewhat dependent on the external environment for their survival needs, abundant game and a good harvest are influenced by natural factors that, for most of our evolution, we didn't fully understand. We need to be able to cooperate with others to have shelter, safety and sustenance beyond the very basics.

A healthy *interdependence*—the mutual reliance between individuals or groups in which each contributes something essential to the functioning or well-being of the other—was necessary for humans to become the advanced species we are: capable of organization, housing and feeding growing societies, making great art and fine wine, building meaningful legacies. Interdependence is a dynamic where no one is entirely self-sufficient, and cooperative relationships are necessary for survival, growth, and thriving—emotionally, materially, and socially.

Building a system of interdependence relies on five core principles:

Mutual Contribution

Everyone has something to offer—skills, knowledge, labor, care, perspective—and these offerings complement and support each other. Think of a village where some farm, some teach, some heal, and all roles are valued.

Reciprocity and Trust

Interdependence thrives on give-and-take over time. It's not transactional in the short-term sense, but more like an evolving balance where people contribute because they trust that others will too.

Shared Goals and Outcomes

Cooperative interdependence means people work together toward outcomes they couldn't achieve alone—such as raising children, building communities, protecting ecosystems, or creating culture.

Vulnerability and Reliability

Being interdependent means accepting some level of vulnerability: allowing others to meet needs we can't meet alone and showing up reliably so others can depend on us in turn.

Individual Autonomy Within Connection

Interdependence doesn't mean enmeshment. Each person maintains their autonomy but recognizes their actions affect others and vice versa. It's distinct from codependence (where boundaries blur) or hyper-independence (where connection is avoided).

That last principle of Individual Autonomy Within Connection is potentially the trickiest piece to navigate in our modern culture of hyper-independence, self-sufficiency, and competition. For many of us, even our closest and most intimate relationships can be pushed away and cordoned off as potential threats to the constructs—usually inherited familiar patterns—we play out to protect ourselves from what we've built. What building a Safe Space will do is help us shift into a state of interdependence, where we are owning our part by first meeting our needs internally before we communicate. We are then able to engage externally from a different place and a different set of objectives.

Self-knowledge is more than merely an awareness of your patterns and the emotional traditions that shaped them. It also resides in taking accountability for yourself.

Managing your responses to the things that occur becomes self-wisdom; alignment is created when people can bring both self-knowledge in the form of awareness and self-wisdom in the form of accountability into a conversation.

Let's return to the mountain. You've arrived at base camp, and you are gazing at the summit far above you. The obstacles and hazards of the mountain are more discernable now that you're closer to it, but the scale of each of the hazards on the mountain's face is hard to determine. Plus, you don't yet have the detail of resolution—sharpness or clarity—necessary to know the nature of the hazards and how to build a strategy to overcome them. You need information.

Fortunately, at base camp there are other climbers, some of whom may have been on the mountain and they could know things about the uniqueness of the mountain's face from their own perspective that will help you strategize your ascent. Building the Safe Space will require three key components: **individual safety, relational safety, and familial safety.**

Individual awareness is something we have been working on, by understanding and mapping your Land of Familiar and identifying the emotional traditions you've inherited. By now, you might have an awareness of the stories you have told yourself about yourself to survive. You might also have mapped out the inherited familiar patterns that may have shaped your life so far, and you have tried to meet your six human needs in unhealthy ways. You likely have created a manifesto that reverses your old stories from the land of Familiar and have identified healthy ways of meeting your six human needs.

You are ready to move onto the next stage of building the Safe Space: creating relational safety. So far, your hard work in developing your individual awareness might have been done alone, without much input from others. To build relational safety, you must now take your individual awareness to the other people in your life, communicate about it and create a way of having difficult conversations that builds trust and understanding.

Building the Safe Space–Relational Safety

Most of us have been merely surviving in the Land of Familiar for our entire lives. We all need to understand that we have choices beyond merely surviving there but not all of us are going through this process of the ascent. Others in our lives may be caught in their own Land of Familiar—stuck in their own inherited patterns just as we have been. It could be that there are people in your life who aren't willing to undergo a process of building individual awareness and resist the work you are doing. Or, it could be that there are people in your life who do want to better understand themselves but are taking a different route using modalities that work better for them.

How do we create a Safe Space for communication? What we seek externally, we lack internally. You have to feel safe with yourself before you can feel safe with other people.

For years, I had been repeating the same behaviors that had kept me in relative safety in my childhood. Based on the beliefs that were so ingrained in me, by taking on all the blame and by taking on the mantle of "the other" my imposter was running the show, not to harm me but to keep me safe in an unsafe environment.

That is what is so challenging about recognizing the impostor and finally taking back the control it has over your life; it can feel like you are tearing down all of the systems that have protected you throughout your life, and that without those systems you will never find safety. This feeling is normal, and in order to overcome it, you must realize that when you deconstruct one system you create an opportunity to design a new one.

I eventually reached a point in my own emotional development where I was "doing different," as a result of becoming different. Consider this quote by an unknown author—probably a motivational speaker: "The road to the meadow of transformation is by meandering through the forest of our feelings."

Any emotional journey will be like navigating the twists, turns and hazards of the woods. The destination isn't always clear. The path isn't always defined. However, by keeping to the determination to get to the other side of those woods, using a set of principles and skills to navigate its pitfalls, seeing the other side becomes possible.

My impostor had protected me by telling me:

- It's my fault.
- I will be punished because it's my fault.
- Any success I have in life—money, status, relationships—has to fit the pattern of it's my fault.

These beliefs had to change by *design*, by choice. I realized I had the knowledge to change yet had not taken action to change. I deliberately stopped being the guy who craved attention and significance.

I decided to stop "othering myself" for the desperation of fitting in and confusing that with belonging. It was only when I chose to give myself permission to feel my feelings, without judging them or trying to analyze them, was when I became truly connected with myself. My Safe Space is connection. When I experience my feelings, I am connected with the little boy in me and not abandoning that little boy through pleasure-seeking distractions,

My journey and desire to create a safer emotional world started when I was in the wealth management industry. I always worked with wealthy families, particularly business owners and their families. I started to see patterns in their emotional dynamics, that even though these individuals had accumulated impressive material wealth, which gave them the illusion of safety, none of them felt emotionally safe with themselves or their families. These individuals were disconnected from their feelings, each other and ultimately from themselves.

In my work with my coach, before creating the concepts of the Land of Familiar, the Impostor, and Safe Space, I had an epiphany. My imposter had prevented me from feeling my feelings. I was disconnected. Because of my childhood, the common and familiar feelings of shame, anger, loneliness, despair and deep loneliness were all I knew, so I made the subconscious decision to numb them, to distract myself from feeling them. My numbing agents of choice—to avoid these mysterious unwanted things called feelings—were, alcohol, womanizing, and consumerism. I had been seeking safety in pleasure and material distraction and yet I was in a deep state of discomfort because that safety was an illusion.

We all want to feel emotionally safe, safe within ourselves, with our relationships and with our resources, whatever they may be. The healthy way to achieve this emotional safety is by reconnecting with ourselves and that is achieved by allowing ourselves to first feel our feelings and then live our feelings in a safe way with others. I choose to embrace Little Chef—my nickname for the little boy in me—and be *with* him, by being *with* the feelings that come, and I mean *all* the feelings, even the ugly ones, like shame.

Compassion for self, connection with self, leads to compassion and connection with others. Understanding oneself, leads to understanding others. I realized that, if I could create the process for myself, maybe I could replicate it in a way that would work for others. In listening to the many stories of my clients and encountering repeating pattern after repeating pattern, it seemed obvious to me that what was lacking was a structured dialogue for excavating these emotional traditions within individuals and within families. Safe Space is about uncovering what we seek externally and lack internally and exploring how we can give that to ourselves. It's about reconnecting with our feelings. Once we are able to connect with our feelings, we are able to connect with others and what they are feeling. This is what led to my creating Veritage and the tools that we use to help clients identify and navigate emotional traditions and design new ones.

We guide them toward emotional governance, governing feelings from your Safe Space, not from a Land of Familiar.

British theater and film director, Peter Brook, known for his surrealist and haunting productions of Jean Cocteau's *The Infernal Machine* and Arthur Miller's *A View from the Bridge*—among hundreds of other plays and films over 60 years—opens his 1968 book *The Empty Space* by writing, "I can take any empty space and call it a bare stage." Brook is saying that theater exists whenever someone performs and someone watches—no elaborate sets or buildings are required; it's the presence of the people involved that creates the experience. Brook, through the course of *The Empty Space* describes different types of theater:

- **Deadly Theater** has become stagnant, conventional, and safe. It repeats old forms without vitality, relying on tradition rather than innovation. Its equivalent in life would be the illusion of safety; the stories we hold to be true and the lies we tell ourselves.

- **Holy Theater** seeks to explore metaphysical, spiritual, or sacred dimensions of human experience. The journey to build the Safe Space is clearly a kind of Holy Theater.

- **Rough Theatre** is raw, entertaining, and immediate. It speaks directly to the audience and often embraces humor, satire, and populism. It's analogous to what happens inside of a Safe Space where we are improvising within a framework. Anything can happen and we build trust by making the connections that keep the dialogue going.

- **Immediate Theater** is the ideal form of theatre, according to Brook. It is present, alive, and responsive to the moment. It relies on a relationship between those on stage and those watching, and **through feeling together they create intimacy, and awareness. They co-create the experience.** This is the Veritage process in a nutshell. Part of the work we do is, we help individuals become self-aware by watching

> the theatre of their life with the lens of curiosity and playfulness, not the lens of judgment and making mistakes .

Like the good doctor assessing his patients, Brook wrote the book as if he were a doctor diagnosing the health of a patient. He identifies symptoms, recalls past remedies, considers alternatives, and proposes a radical cure: Create an encounter that matters.

Creating a Safe Space isn't theatre but it relies on some of the same principles that Brook employs to illustrate an ideal of Immediate Theater in that Safe Spaces are co-created by everyone in the room and only if a Safe Space remains committed to the truth of the moment and the humanity of its participants.

Questions to ponder:

1. How can you separate your role as parent/child from your role as an adult in other areas of your life?

2. What are three ways you have habitually focused on mere survival?

3. How have each of these survival habits impacted your relationships—with yourself, and others?

4. No one family is "fine." What are the unhelpful family traditions you're not acknowledging in your own family?

5. Which of these emotional traditions are you fine with?

6. Which of these emotional traditions disturb you?

7. Which of these emotional traditions are you emotionally uncertain or insecure about?

8. How are your feelings about these emotional traditions showing up for you, physically and emotionally?

CHAPTER 11

Setting the Stage

Parents set the stage for what their children will become as adults. Parents do this by modelling emotional traditions through their behaviors and especially through their communication. The transmission of ideas, thoughts and feelings between human beings is perhaps the single most important aspect of our development as a species.

Yet humans can take communication entirely for granted. We speak, write, text, and gesticulate—rarely pausing to fully consider the effect of evolution on the act. Yet, human communication, especially through language, is one of the most complex, fragile, artful, and significant advancements our species has developed. And we treat it as ordinary. We assume words will function, that others will understand what we intend and mean, that our meanings will carry across the vast internal chasms between us. But verbal communication is not a guarantee of mutual understanding. Throughout time, it has failed spectacularly. And when communication does fail, the consequences could shatter intimate moments of connection, ripple through history, and even bring down civilizations. Communication isn't just a feature of human life—it *helps sustain* human life. We build civilizations with it. We end wars with it. We fall in love, come undone, and find our way back to each other.

By definition, communication is transmitting information, thoughts, or feelings from one entity to another through a shared system of symbols, signs, and behaviors. During more than two million years of evolution on Earth, humans have learned to communicate. It is what has enabled us to cooperate: hunt, trade, fight, and give birth to great works of art, among other achievements. It is something that, if we don't master it, might render even the most brilliant genius completely unable to actualize their genius in a tangible and meaningful way.

By around age five, children generally have learned to understand 4,000–6,000 words. By age six, most children have a personal vocabulary of around 10,000 words. That rate of language absorption translates to about 6-10 new words every day, but communication isn't just about memorizing words—it's about mapping those words onto sometimes complex feelings, relationships, categories, concepts and sensory experiences. It is both a semantic (symbolic) and somatic (bodily) fusion of concept, association and feeling happening at a speed measured in milliseconds—the speed it takes for a sensation to traverse the nervous system and reach the human brain. Children are learning new words simply by being in the world—they are like sponges absorbing what they come into contact with.

Let's say a child feels something like acute hunger, frustration, or joy and that feeling creates a bodily expression, crying, raging, or maybe hugging. These are innate behaviors that many animals share in common. Humans are something different in that, as a child grows up, their caregivers automatically observe their child's bodily expressions and blurt out a word to describe it—"Oh! You're hungry, aren't you?" or "You broke your toy! You must be so upset!" Parents don't realize it in the moment, but this is what behavioral scientists call *co-regulation*, naming the feeling while mirroring the child's internal state—soothing touch, eye contact, moments of joint attention, taking turns talking. We do it all the time and we hardly ever think about it any more than we would think about breathing.

Generally, over the first six years of a child's life and through repetition, this co-regulation cycle will play out tens of thousands of times, day-after-day and by the time that child is old enough—typically between the ages of three and five—the child has symbolically internalized around 10,000 of these word–feeling associations that were modeled for them by their co-regulating parents or caregivers. That sounds like a tremendous amount of work, and it is but it's work we do naturally and have been doing for millions of years.

The affective labeling of embodied concepts and the language used to describe them is blended and, over time eventually helps form our map of reality. Without this automatic process of mirroring and association, we wouldn't be able to communicate or function in the world very well. The difference across cultures and especially between families lies in which feelings are labeled, which cues are emphasized and which rules around emotional expression are normalized.

"Difficult" topics such as understanding emotions are often not taught as a life skill or a discipline until much later in life and even then, when we as adults do seek out specific methods of communication. The way we will apply those methods isn't necessarily universal. We feel, but don't necessarily learn to discuss what we feel beyond the plainest expression of the word or gesture we use to describe the feeling—*I feel angry. I am upset.* Descriptions of our feelings are an important starting point, but they aren't capable of being much more than declarations of a fact. Even when we grow into adults, when we do describe a feeling by naming it, we might still be operating as children do by expecting others to do something about the feeling—we externalize what we could be giving to ourselves.

When we externalize how we get our needs met—and the feelings we attach to them— we're likely to keep ourselves stuck in inherited familiar patterns. When we're in that state, we might not necessarily be able to understand that we're operating in a pattern, let alone be able to make sense of it or make sense of anyone else's.

The Emotional Anatomy of Collapse

Today, in our era of smart phones and jet travel, it's easy for us to regard our distant ancestors the way we might think of aliens, or cave men—as something vaguely familiar but completely different. We might tend to think of ourselves as being somehow better and more evolved than people of the past because of the many social and technological advances that have been made over hundreds and thousands of years, advances that enable us to live lives of increasingly greater relative opportunity and comfort when compared to the "brutish, nasty and short" lives our ancient progenitors lived. But, while the world around us has changed, and our ability to be masters of nature and to build more equitable societies has increased, there is one thing that hasn't changed in millions of years: the human nervous system and how it responds to communication, especially in childhood.

While there have been movements in psychology that understood that how we communicate with our children sets the stage for who they become. For example, Rudolf Steiner's Waldorf School in the early twentieth century and Dr. Benjamin McLane Spock's parenting methods in the 1940s give us blueprints that allow us to predict the future because the human nervous system was much the same in the past as it is now. If we can understand these past emotional dynamics and build effective tools to govern them, we might be able to better resolve conflicts, increase human functioning and better preserve the legacy of our families, businesses, institutions, nations and other social groups.

How a child is raised can have a profound impact on that child's effect on others. That child's ability to gain a position of influence or leadership in adulthood can, depending on the emotional dynamics of their childhood—and the child's ability to understand those dynamics—create good times and it can create bad times.

Let's say your father was a monarch in the thirteenth century. A king was expected to lead his men in the vanguard on horseback facing the same degree of danger as his knights and men-at-arms. The king, who it was believed had been appointed by God as the ruler by divine right—was the emotional anchor for the men at his back; if he fell in battle, the resulting emotional blow could reduce the orderly ranks of men fighting under him into a desperate rout.

Like a small child being handed a suit of armor he can't lift—told by his father that, "This is what love, respect, and legitimacy look like," while being physically and temperamentally unable to bear it, an heir to the throne in that time might internalize his father's standard but not be able to embody it. The result might have been nothing short of chronic dissonance, shame and a fractured identity. Internal desires and innate abilities might not match the heavy emotional coat of armor being placed on the heir.

Re-Setting the Stage

How do parents who want to set the stage for the next generation's success end up trashing their legacy because the "coat of armor" they put on their heirs is ill-fitting and/or too heavy? They try to force the child to fit the armor, to square their shoulders and handle the weight.

A typical pattern of behavior of parents in families with entrenched negative emotional traditions is to keep their children at arm's length while they are young. The child will get glimpses into the adult world their parents inhabit and the emotional dynamics that operate day-to-day, but that's it. Then, one day, adulthood—that heavy, ill-fitting coat of armor—is dumped on them. The responsibility of running an entire life complete with responsibilities, duties, obligations, costs and relationships is now in their lap.

Seems overwhelming? It is.

In most families, the people I work with are keenly aware of the pressure that comes with running things. Specifically in families, the parents' desire to prepare their children for taking over responsibility for their own lives typically leads them to push a child into a narrowly defined path to competency. Through formal education, parents may think they are preparing their kids by enrolling them in an MBA program and giving them all the tactical tools to thrive. But an MBA without emotional preparedness is not going to get you through the most challenging moments in your life.

By the time our children are adults—or very nearly adults—and old enough to even be considered, we likely have already set the stage for their emotional reality, and we will have done that largely unconsciously through being in our own Land of Familiar and all the emotional patterns that characterize it. We can't wipe the slate clean and start over again from zero, building word-concept associations from scratch. That groundwork—however positively or negatively—was done by the time our children were young

According to findings from Veritage's 2026 *The Missing Link in Family Business Transitions: How Emotional Disconnection Threatens Family Legacy* research report, preparedness for ownership and wealth transition can be fraught with emotional challenges. Among those surveyed, the Founder/Current Owner generation identified the top two emotional challenges in their family as 1) Rivalry and 2) Entitlement. When the same question was asked to the next generation members, their top two answers were 1) Communication (or lack thereof) and 2) Control. It would not be a stretch to say that both generations are pointing at each other when it comes to emotional challenges in the family. So, how have they structured themselves to address these challenges? Well, 55 percent of Founder/Current Owners and 41 percent of Next Gens said that their families have a governance document that deals with succession and wealth transfer. When both generations were asked if their existing governance documents address the emotional issues and family dynamics, 64 percent of Founder/Current Owners and 76 percent of Next Gens said they do not. This is leading to a situation where more than two out of every three next generation members surveyed do not see a clear path mapped out for them to take over ownership and wealth decisions. Unfortunately, only 12 percent of survey respondents said that they work with a professional on family dynamics issues so these issues are not being actively dealt with and that risks the future legacy of what has been built and who will be involved.

We can identify a few key **metrics of emotional preparedness** relevant to all families, no matter their resources, when navigating generational role transitions. This research shows that both children stepping into adulthood and adults shifting their role in the family dynamic often fail to develop and design certain emotional capacities:

Emotional Self-Regulation and Identity.

This includes the ability to manage one's own emotions, so they benefit, not hinder, the family system. They also include breaking emotional patterns and false equations that uphold a negative emotional tradition. Just as importantly, both have to define and develop acceptance of one's own identity and role in the family, beyond status, money, or the function they serve in the family system. This depends upon awareness of belief patterns and behaviors that influence decisions.

Emotional Safety and Communication. The capacity of families having structured, regular conversations about feelings, goals, and challenges utilizing a Safe Space to communicate difficult information openly, respectfully, and consistently. Instead of relying on avoidance or ignoring emotional information, these families can design systems to express one's feelings and thoughts without fear of judgment or retaliation.

Trust and Control Dynamics. Families that have developed mutual trust between generations in decision-making; this includes parents and adults in the family dynamic being able to let go of control without feeling a loss of identity, as well as children and young adults being trusted to step up without being over-managed or excluded.

Inclusion. Young adults and the next generation are included in governance, planning, and decision-making in a way that recognizes their unique contribution and perspective. Equal opportunity for all members to be heard, regardless of hierarchy, age, role, or personality.

Resilience and Emotional Preparedness. The ability to balance internal performance pressures with realistic expectations. Awareness of how the family legacy—its demands, expectations, or inherited social roles—create stress, anxiety, or mental health challenges.

Family Relational Trust. Families that address unresolved conflicts, generational trauma, or patterns through a system of emotional governance (such as a Safe Space) rather than passing them on. This also includes families that have engaged in Safe Space conversations about fairness, belonging, and history; respecting rather than criticizing; supporting instead of competing.

Adaptability, Responsibility and Stewardship. Families that have designed a "stewardship mindset." Parents and adults see one's role as temporary, with the important responsibility to pass things on in due time and through a process of preparedness—including emotional preparedness. Children that step into adulthood with gratitude and readiness to evolve the family legacy, especially its emotional legacy.

The key to preparing the next generation for an adulthood of emotional preparedness is to include them from the beginning in a positive emotional tradition.

Look at how responsibilities within the family change as we grow older: human and social capital, relationship and household management, caregiving and stewardship traditions. Consider what kind of family agreements, boundaries, and rituals you have, whether they have been articulated or not. For example, who makes decisions, how conflicts are resolved, when and how family talks in a Safe Space happen. As for the last one, building the Safe Space will reset the stage.

Questions to ponder:

1. What is your entitled brat entitled to emotionally and what recurring patterns might you be creating in your life to meet that emotional need?

2. How might your entitled brat be different if its emotional needs had been acknowledged rather than suppressed?

3. Can you parent effectively if you seek emotional validation from your children?

4. How might your potential be crushed by your own emotional inheritance?

5. How does unprocessed grief for a parent shape the way you connect emotionally with others?

CHAPTER 12

Hugging the Ugly

Our earliest ancestors did not stand alone—they joined forces in small tribes to survive. Our human consciousness was shaped by our connections to people closest proximity to us. We found safety in numbers and were united not by what made us different, but what made us similar.

Acceptance into a tribe roots you in a community outside of your immediate kinship, a family outside of the family. But at the core of tribalism exists a paradox: Humans can end up being deeply connected to some, while at the same time being completely disconnected from others.

Tribes demand loyalty and while they can offer the security of belonging in return, they can also foster an us-versus-them mentality. So, just as our emotional need to be accepted by members of a particular group is intrinsic, perhaps the answer to finding our true belonging lies within ourselves and not in others.

Somewhere along the way we began to form tribes that were less about survival and more about satisfying our need to belong, defining our sense of self and social identity. Groups help us answer the existentially significant question, "Who am I?"

The self is not just a "me," but also a "we," hence why we may tend to bond most naturally with those who are like us. For better or for worse, this strong tendency to bond through affiliation might closely connect us to an emotional tradition that greatly enhances our chances of survival. It could also tie us to a set of traits that the tribe considers preferable, such as reason, compassion, ambition, strength, or even certain forms of physical and social desirability, and we could develop those traits within ourselves and perform them in healthy ways. Conversely, if we haven't faced our impostor, we might be compelled to pursue those same traits (and others like them) in unhealthy ways. The pursuit of desirable traits is motivated by the need to be accepted by the tribe, thus guaranteeing survival. One of the world's longest studies of adult development that began at Harvard in 1938 during the Great Depression, found that close relationships, more than money or fame, keep people happy throughout their lives. These healthy connections protect people from life's discontents, help delay mental and physical decline, and are good predictors of long and happy lives. The same research team also found that those raised in warmer family environments were more securely attached to their partners in the later years of life—a testament to the enduring influence of early childhood experiences.

So, while it is readily accepted that we all have this basic need to belong, many of us confuse the ways in which we attempt to achieve this connection. American professor and best-selling author Dr. Brené Brown defines belonging in her 2010 book *The Gifts of Imperfection* as: "the innate human desire to be part of something larger than us." She describes it as a powerful primal yearning to fit in, but in the attempt, instead of finding belonging, we erect barriers to it. Here is the conclusion: "true belonging only happens when we present our authentic, imperfect selves to the world, our sense of belonging can never be greater than our level of self-acceptance." (p.26)

When you try to fit in instead of actually belonging, you mold yourself to the situation or circumstance you are in. You compromise your truth by projecting a version of yourself that you assume to be more appealing and attractive. This provides a false sense of safety totally absent from real connection, and in turn you might end up feeling lonelier than if you had shown up as your authentic self.

So, how do you know when you belong and when you are merely fitting in? Well, you are most likely to feel it because being incongruent to who you truly are feels like hard work. It's like being in a constant state of battle with yourself whereby you end up hiding parts of yourself in exchange of acceptance from another—acceptance over which you have no control.

For as far back as she can remember, writer and journalist Laura Hearn had this aching feeling that she didn't fit in. Quiet and shy by nature, she was the epitome of a "good girl." Struggling with the divorce of her parents at a young age, she desperately craved the attention and love of her father. Without the awareness and space to express her emotions safely, Laura retreated into her own make-believe world.

But despite having a physical safe place to call home, Laura felt entirely unsafe in her own skin. Bullied throughout school for being the chubby kid, she felt ugly on both the inside and outside. Seeking comfort, she would raid the fridge and kitchen cupboards as soon as she walked through the door, only to feel disgust and shame at her body immediately after.

Looking back, it was clear that Laura was suffering in silence, but it took just one moment to change the course of her life forever.

One night on the way home from work, Laura's stepfather was killed in a car crash. In the immediate aftermath of his death, and while those around her were struggling to process what had happened, Laura failed to show any of the usual symptoms associated with loss. Almost without hesitation, she packed her bags and embarked on a gap year in Australia. But six months into her trip, the delayed grief caught up with her and she rapidly became entrenched in the cycle of deceit that prevails an eating disorder.

She returned home completely unaware of what was happening to her, and with little awareness of anorexia, her mom and sister were both clueless and powerless to help. Anorexia became Laura's safe place; it gave her a sense of power, an identity and a way to escape the painful emotions that she was ill-equipped to cope with. The only place outside of her anorexia that gave her some relief and a sense of belonging was at the stables. The horses never judged her and accepted her as she was in that very moment–something she was unable to do for herself. An eating disorder thrives in isolation and is an excruciatingly lonely place to be. Full of self-doubt and self-loathing, Laura removed herself from the world, living her life on the periphery of others.

Without access to the right support, she spent over a decade of her life in and out of treatment, feeling hopeless that she would never find another way to live. It was only when a therapist gave her a book written by a clinician acclaimed for her expertise in the eating disorder field, that Laura finally felt understood, seen and heard. Scared, but also desperate, she spent eight months at a clinic learning how to process the multitude of emotions her eating disorder had so expertly numbed. The feeling of not being good enough, the unprocessed grief surrounding her stepfather, the shame and self-loathing was laid bare. The ugliness of her eating disorder could hide no more.

Laura is often asked what it was about her time in the clinic that helped her to heal when everything before had failed. "I felt like someone finally spoke my language" She says in a 2024 interview for this book, "Many of the staff had recovered themselves, and were unafraid to hold my eating disorder to account. It was the first time I learnt what it meant to feel emotionally safe. I didn't feel quite so ugly anymore."

Laura developed her eating disorder long before the infiltration of social media entered our lives. The internet has removed the barriers of geography, meaning anyone with internet access can connect anywhere in the world. Finding "belonging" ought never to be easier. But while social media has at many levels increased knowledge and inclusion, it has paradoxically created ignorance and exclusion, both of which have been abused for financial gain.

There is a long history of high-profile individuals influencing consumer buying decisions dating back to the eighteenth century, when a potter named Josiah Wedgwood created a tea set for Queen Charlotte. With the royal stamp of approval, he capitalized on his status as potter to Her Majesty by marketing his Queen's Ware range to the mass market. Fast forward to the early 2000s with the introduction of social media platforms such as Facebook and Instagram, and we can chart the trajectory and rise of the kind of influencers we are familiar with today.

The American author Seth Godin in his 2008 book *Tribes: We need you to lead us* classifies this loyal group of people who are connected to a common cause as "consumer tribes." The internet has created an evolution of content creators who tap into these groups by luring consumers through similar values and interests. Social media influencers feel more relatable and accessible than their Hollywood counterparts—and with the convenience of technology everyone has the opportunity to become one. Consumer tribes have in many ways transcended the old ties of ancestral kinship, becoming an extension of our inner circle. With a younger population often feeling unheard, misrepresented and disillusioned, they offer an alternative place to "belong."

British social psychologist Henri Tajfel's 1970s social identity theory, explains how individuals create and define their place in society by viewing themselves as belonging to groups and adopting their values and behaviors to fit in. By buying a certain product used by a favorite content creator, we automatically feel as though we are one of the tribe. Some creators have become so highly desirable that they demand huge fees for a single post. At 25, Kylie Jenner became the world's most followed woman on Instagram. With 378 million followers, she reportedly was paid around $1.2 million per Instagram post. Eye-watering numbers by all accounts, but how did she get here?

As the youngest member of the famous Kardashian-Jenner family, Kylie was surrounded by numerous famous faces from a young age. Making her appearance on the reality TV show at fourteen years old, she shared her life under the glare of the world alongside her parents and siblings. Kylie's success was of course helped by the fame and power of her family, but she also tapped into the millions of impressionable young girls on social media by using her own image to promote her products. In 2014 and with a vast following, Kylie Cosmetics was launched, becoming an instant hit with her Instagram followers. Young girls all over the world saw "perfect" images of her pouting with her Kylie Jenner Lip Kit, hanging out with her boyfriend or posing for selfies, and wanted to be her.

While many celebrities originally dominated Instagram, it didn't take long for micro bloggers to start producing specific content to build their own following. TV networks also saw the potential to grow their audience, and thus reality TV formats were born, providing another space to form communities. The British dating game show *Love Island*, which now has more than twenty versions worldwide is the perfect example. Audiences unite in the discourse surrounding the characters and connect with one another on open forums such as X, Instagram and TikTok.

But wealth, fame and all the trappings that come with it can serve as a great mask for deep rooted insecurities and can lead to devastating consequences. Hana Kimura, a professional Japanese wrestler who appeared in the Netflix reality TV show *Terrace House* gained enormous attention as a public figure in Japan. In the episode called "The Case of the Costume Incident," Hana lost her temper at fellow housemate Kai Kobayashi when he accidentally shrunk her expensive wrestling costume in the washing machine. Hana's costume was one of her most treasured possessions and acted as a barrier between her authentic self and the public persona that had become her identity. Without her costume, Hana's vulnerability was exposed under the glare of the world. With her emotions left wide open, the anger she expressed towards Kobayashi became a target for abuse and harassment on social media. Only months after leaving the show on the 23rd of May 2020, Hana was found dead at her home in Tokyo with a number of suicide notes. The stream of online hate she received about her appearance and behavior on the show, prompted calls for the government to take more action against anonymous social media users who post abusive content.

The immense pressure on the young to bend their faces and souls out of shape in the pursuit of living their best life is evident. These so-called influencers prop up the illusion of a perfect self in the pursuit of "belonging." They feed the facade that you can make money without ever leaving your bedroom–that "although you are not like me, you could be if you join my tribe."

Our roadmap for healthy relationships in our adult life begins as soon as we are born. Babies whose needs are met such as feeding, changing and soothing are able to form an attachment. When infants receive unconditional love, acceptance and safety from their primary caregivers, they learn to trust the outside world, have a greater sense of self-esteem and don't feel the need to fit in.

A number of people in the financial community have long thought of me as a very successful family business coach. But the belief "I didn't belong in that tribe" had been formed from a young age. For years, I avoided confrontation and uncomfortable conversations; living inauthentically became torturous. Expensive toys and a cellar full of vintage wine did nothing but provide a temporary mask to hide my internal conflict. Creating the illusion of wealth was all part of my pursuit of validation, acceptance and belonging.

Life felt fake, but I was afraid of what might surface if I confronted the imposter and removed the mask. Who would want or love me if they knew who I really was? It took one person to see all of him without judgment to begin a transformation. I began to look inside myself for answers. We all create false equations that can run our lives. They arise out of the patterns we experience and the emotional traditions that are modeled for us. My false equation was: Love = Sex = Connection = Shame, therefore, Love = Shame. Knowing that my shame from childhood made me feel unsafe in expressing honest thoughts, feelings, and opinions as an adult, I actively sought the building blocks of a Safe Space. What needed to come together to make it possible for me to throw off self-imposed limits on intimacy and embrace vulnerability as a strength? It took a mentor for me to see all of Franco Lombardo—the good, the bad, *and* the ugly.

While we all have unique qualities, many of us negate the value of them and instead choose to focus on our flaws, or the negative side of uniqueness. Afraid to show up warts and all, we create another beautifully crafted Instagram post, appear on a reality TV show, buy another car or escape into the confines of an eating disorder. But the security that we gain from outside sources in order to belong is fragile and fleeting. At some point in our lives, people will reject us, businesses will fail, and relationships will end. So, while the Western world sustains a constant appetite for consumerism in search of belonging, there are those who focus less on the competition and more on community.

Jane Marindany, aka "Mama Jane" grew up in the poor village of Emori Joi, Kenya, and just like her peers, she had to master balancing heavy jugs of water on her head almost as soon as she had taken her first steps. Taken out of school in the third grade and married with five children at a young age, she was destined to lead the same life of poverty as her parents and grandparents before her.

Then, she opened her eyes to that community and started to see possibilities, sharing in her interview, "I started by taking my tea without sugar—saving 50 shillings a week. It doesn't sound much but everything I have today began with sacrificing the sweetness in my tea, for a sweeter tomorrow."

Today Mama Jane is one of her community's leading entrepreneurs providing much of her family's income through a cooperative of village women, who make and sell intricate beaded jewelry. She has also, with the help of her community, built their first school where Mama Jane and her five children are educated and given the opportunity to create a different life for themselves.

Mama Jane's journey to being admired as a leader in her community and further afield didn't happen by accident. It required her to show up at her most vulnerable and be unapologetic in rejecting calls for her to fit in. Determined to build a better future for herself and her family from the one that had been mapped out, she chose community over competition. In the absence of wanting to measure up to anyone else's idea of beauty, success, or worthiness, Mama Jane was free to be herself and create a safe space for others to do the same. Her reward was far more than a sweeter tasting cup of tea: it was a life that as a girl she had only dreamed of. A life full of beauty that radiated from her internal compass.

The lengths many of us go to avoid being who we truly are can manifest in many ways. To rid ourselves of our perceived "ugliness" we build walls around ourselves to prevent anyone from catching a glimpse of who we really are. Not just associated with the aesthetic, our moral character and mental capacity are left wide open for judgement and scrutiny in a modern world that fears a sense of otherness. It's no wonder that many of us feel unsafe in a society that condemns "different."

The late Italian essayist and philosopher Umberto Eco said that beauty is boring, since it must follow certain rules, whereas ugliness is unpredictable and offers a range of possibilities.

So, what if we chose to reimagine where we find our sense of belonging? What if we began with ourselves first and embraced the very parts of us that we perpetually hide. What if we chose to acknowledge all our flaws as part of being human—the feelings and emotions that we bury deep in the fabric of our core. What if we stopped giving our power away to people, places and things and brought it back home?

So much of our story lies in the narrative that we tell ourselves—the lies, the shame, the ugly truths that we shut out in favor of presenting a beautifully curated version. But to find belonging with others, we must first find it with ourselves. In this fractured world that can at times feel like an ideological combat zone, we must first have the courage to stand alone, before we can stand with another. Mama Jane didn't look to others to find her place in the world; she did so by trusting in her own convictions. She knew the value in both "being with" and "being alone."

Humans will never cease wanting to be part of something, but we need it to be real, not conditional, fake or compromised. The first thing we must do is hug the ugly parts of ourselves, face who we really are and honor our imperfections without exception.

I met Jeremy at a speaking event I did for an institution in Canada. The successful founder of a property development and investment company, Jeremy is also the father of six grown adult children who all work in the business.

Immediately I noticed Jeremy was incredibly charismatic, driven and forthcoming in expressing his love for his family. We chatted after the event, and I agreed to assist Jeremy with his family dynamics challenges. He had shared an incident with his oldest son where they ended up being physically abusive with each other.

Jeremy shared how the experience left him feeling sad and that he desperately wanted to repair the relationship with his children. He also admitted that although the business was very successful and was generating a healthy profit, the family (which Jeremy claimed mattered to him) was deeply unhealthy.

Believing that he was doing the "right" thing, Jeremy had put in place a mechanism to assist him with the transfer of the wealth and ownership to the next generation. He hired an advisor that reported to him and acted as the go between him and his children, hopeful that having a non-family executive in place would be a good idea.

While this seemed like a good idea on paper, it didn't materialize in real life. When I interviewed the children, they all expressed their frustration that although their father had appointed a non-family executive, he was still very much involved in the decision making and operations. When I challenged Jeremy about this, he said that all he was doing was to try and "advise" his children, even though they had never asked him to. The tension that Jeremy's interfering created was the catalyst for the fight that I mentioned earlier with his eldest son, the CEO of the firm.

During a coaching session, Jeremy shared a story that when he was nine years old, he got lost coming home from school. As we began to unpack the experience, it became evident that the incident introduced significant trauma into Jeremy's life and had caused him to have less trust in himself. The result was that he felt a constant need to control situations due to his inability to trust anyone—even himself. The terror of not being able to find his way home had haunted him.

Jeremy repeatedly self-sabotaged by setting others up for failure, so that he could play the hero role and save the day. I invited

Jeremy to be brave, dive deeper and explore all the areas of life where his pattern was showing up. He realized that his "ugly" was getting in the way of him showing his family how much he really did love them and had alienated his children to the point where they had in some cases pulled away completely from him.

Unfortunately, Jeremy was not able to fully "hug his ugly" and I had to make the difficult decision to disengage from working with him and his family. The day I told him I would be ceasing our work together, I was deeply saddened, but it was a lesson in my own growth journey; I realized I cannot help those that are not capable or unwilling to help themselves.

Human beings, me included, are great at making excuses, justifying and not taking full accountability for our behaviors. We are experts at blaming our parents, siblings, society and every external fact under the sun to avoid taking an honest look at ourselves. One of the oldest continuing forms of self-help we have around the world is the 12-step program.

Formed in 1935 as a wave of alcoholism swept North America during the Great Depression, Bill Wilson and Dr. Bob Smith founded the first Alcoholics Anonymous group in Akron, Ohio. For 90 years the 12-steps of Alcoholics Anonymous have been adapted for 12-step programs centered around many addictions, from debt to relational addiction, to co-dependency. The reason these programs work, in my opinion, is because the first step, "We admitted we are powerless over [our addiction] and our lives have become unmanageable," is active acknowledgment of the reality of the situation.

In hugging my ugly, my shame and my feeling dirty and unwanted involved taking a "no excuses approach" to my current reality. This meant that I could take full accountability for the behaviors

I had employed, the patterns I felt entitled to and the impact I had on myself and others. I had been using the excuses:

- I have it all together.
- I am damaged because of my childhood.
- I am wanted and loved only for what I can provide.

I had to first identify and then examine the impact these excuses were having on myself and my relationships. I had to acknowledge I had been lying to myself and face the carnage I had caused through my treatment (abandonment) of the little boy in me. I had to take ownership of how I had broken trust, caused massive hurt, broken promises, pushed people away and ultimately created what I had feared the most: not being wanted. I had to be compassionately honest with myself—here is the key—*without judgment* of myself.

Only through extreme ownership of the fact that I had been willfully lying to myself by pretending to be someone I am not to avoid feeling the pain of shame and being unwanted, I had lived the life of the imposter. I recalled being alone in a hotel room awash in the pain and anguish my actions had caused someone I loved deeply. I had to embrace the shame, feel it at my core. I had to feel the effects of my actions, and I had to take extreme ownership of the pain I had caused others. Then I had to choose to do differently.

This was me hugging the ugly instead of pushing it away.

I no longer wanted to avoid or numb the shame. I needed, wanted to feel it, be with it, and here is the most important thing: accept it without judgment or excuses.

A critical part of the journey to the summit and a key component for maintaining the summit is the active deconstruction of your default identity, what you feel entitled to, emotionally; to uncover the emotional addiction and emotional traditions which contributed to the repeatable patterns. Once you have unearthed these components of your being you can now intentionally design your new identity away from the impostor based on what matters most to you.

What mattered most to me was creating a safer world by being the model of transformation, as Gandhi says, be the change you would like to see.

My own personal journey has taught me that once I hug my ugly, I am free from the grip it has on me, and I am rewarded with choice—the choice to choose my behaviors instead of my "ugly" choosing them for me. Change doesn't happen all at once. Finding a starting point makes the process feel more achievable. It took me years to identify, let alone hug, my ugly but once I did, my life transformed. I found joy, peace and stillness. Not everyone finds the magic that comes from embracing our "ugly" parts, but the truth is we all have them, and if we use them as opportunities for learning they can be our most powerful tool.

Questions to ponder:

1. Where do you still emotionally struggle in your life?

2. What could be bigger than the shame of staying in your ugly?

3. What behaviors do you keep repeating and want to stop, yet don't know how?

4. What unhelpful beliefs and behaviors are you repeating?

5. What specific emotions or thoughts are you trying to avoid? Why do they feel so threatening to face?

6. With the stories you've read in mind, answer a few questions about your "ugly":
   - Identifying the exact feelings or memories can help bring clarity to what's causing resistance.
   - How does avoiding these parts of yourself impact your relationships, choices, and overall well-being?
   - Suppressing emotions often affects your behavior in ways you may not realize.
   - What fears or beliefs do you hold about confronting these aspects of yourself?
   - Sometimes, the fear of facing certain emotions makes you feel weak.
   - How would your life be different if you accepted and worked through these emotions rather than suppressing them?
   - Imagining a future where you embrace self-awareness can motivate you to change.
   - What small, manageable steps can you take to start acknowledging and processing these parts of yourself?

CHAPTER 13
Dynasty

We all have to face the fact that endings are inevitable. When we find ourselves facing one it could feel like there is nothing beyond it except for oblivion, that the most meaningful things we have done, built, or achieved are behind us. It doesn't come naturally for humans to think of endings as transitions from one state to another state. This idea of endings, whether the end of a king's reign, the ending of adolescence and the beginning of manhood—or womanhood—or most inescapably, the ending of life itself, the finality of it can be overwhelming. If we are still operating as the impostor, we might do everything we possibly can to delay, cheat and avoid an ending.

Most human cultures were surrounded by endings that they could neither prevent nor understand. A famine could destroy crops, a flood might wash away entire villages, great fires might consume towns and those are just a few of the common disasters dealt to human civilizations by mother nature. The manmade ones are obvious. To cope with these grand external forces that were entirely beyond our control, we needed a way of assigning meaning and significance to these events.

The earliest myth-makers—philosophers, religious leaders, and of course the artists were the first to propose that an ending is purposeful and merely a transition between states. They constructed elaborate mythology and symbolic associations with natural disasters, mortality, political change and the ending of social cycles. These patterns are so deeply baked into how we move through the world as a species that we have a yearning for them in our lives and some cultures have managed to hold on to a system of mythology and ritual to mark the ending of one thing and the beginning of another.

One of the oldest examples of a human construct to mark the transition in a closed and repeating cycle of time is the *Ouroboros*—a circular symbol depicting a snake eating its own tail—that can be found in nearly every culture on Earth. The earliest known example of the Ouroboros was found in mysterious desert ruins Egypt dated to around 1600 BCE.

Far to the West, in the moistened jungles of India, we can find on countless Hindu shrines the Kalachakra, the "wheel of time," depicting the human experience of time as a cycle of era or *Yugas* that repeat endlessly and each coming with its own set of challenges, themes and characteristics.

Similar systems of mythology, measuring time and assigning meaning to the changing cycles can be found across the world because, for both agriculture and social organization, humans want to be able to track the seasons with a degree of certainty. But why would human cultures attach mythological significance to the changing of the seasons? Why develop so many rituals, festivals and rites around marking transition?

Because humans see big life changes, such as birth and death, as both disruptive and generative. The change introduces uncertainty, but the rituals offer predictability.

In this chapter, we're focused on your part in creating a dynasty of sorts, that is, a succession within your family that gives each member a sense of prominence and contribution. Unless you have shared practices that reflect and engender healthy connections, the dynasty could collapse as soon as a major change occurs—like the death of a mom or dad.

So, what is the process of developing a new set of emotional traditions that can become the building blocks of a dynasty? In observing and working with families I have noticed there are three assumptions many parents make.

The First Assumption is that all members of the next generation will preserve the family's legacy regardless of their level of interest, or their individual merit. This might include the family's legacy in a profession, for example. You come from three generations of doctors, so you will also be a doctor.

The Second Assumption is that the children or next generation will want to participate in the emotional traditions of the family.

The Third Assumption is that there are no negative family dynamics operating within the family—all of the emotional issues and conflicts have either been resolved, or that there are no emotional issues to resolve.

Ignoring any or all of these three assumptions, failing to discuss them in the context of a Safe Space, as we've discussed in previous chapters, allows them to remain assumptions; succession in the form of children growing into adults will bring up to the surface anything that is unresolved, or suppressed within the family dynamic. All the emotions, all the blocks, all the patterns, and unhealthy ways we meet our needs will show up—and we will have no way of dealing with them. A "dynasty" is impossible without enduring connections.

Change and succession are inevitable. Sooner or later, transitions come, whether we feel prepared for them or not. The task of facing each of the Three Assumptions is not an easy one. Ideally, the younger members of a family or group are gradually included in the responsibilities, values, and traditions that shape the family or group's way of life—but that doesn't always happen. Doubts and anxieties about readiness, willingness, or capacity might cause the older generation to hold back, avoiding difficult conversations.

For those who have hesitated or kept the next generation at a distance, there is still a path forward. It begins with the ascent—understanding the emotional traditions and behavioral patterns that shaped you—and then designing a Safe Space to share these reflections openly with other members of the family. Within that Safe Space, families can notice how the old emotional traditions show up, how they affect relationships, and how each member sees themselves in connection with the group's future. This design process is about preparing the next generation emotionally.

It is about building your dynasty.

As part of this process, the older generation must face another reality: as the next generation succeeds in leading their own lives (of leading the group), they will inevitably do things differently. Continuity is important—not just in what is done, but in why it is done. The meaning and values carried forward may not look identical, but they can be co-created. Some traditions might be preserved, while others might be adapted or replaced entirely to meet the pressures of new times.

Change is the nature of transition. Standards, values, and practices shift with each generation. Just as every age reimagines its own vision of the future, the next generation must feel ownership of what they are building. This can create disagreements, but honest, respectful conversations in a safe space allow empathy to grow between generations. Most importantly, members within families and groups need tolerance for one another during these moments. Neither side has done this before. Even if you were once the younger generation and now find yourself in the older generation's role, it is still new. Everyone is learning. Cut yourself some slack and know that not everything has to be aligned exactly as it was before. That means mistakes will happen, old patterns will be questioned, and new emotional traditions will be made. This is how a living legacy continues—not through rigid preservation, but through the courage to let each generation reshape it for the future.

Designing the Future of the Family

Designing your individual identity with intentionality to overcome and override your human natural tendency to revert back to the Land of Familiar—the landscape of emotional traditions of the past—is a challenging undertaking. It can also be one of the most rewarding things you ever do for your family's emotional future.

Over time, the description of an Emotional Governance Pathway has emerged as part of our work at Veritage. We develop a set of guiding principles unique to each family based on their past emotional traditions; we think of each as the antidote to one negative emotional tradition of your family's past.

At Veritage, what has made our work with families unique is that we don't just identify the guiding principles, we help determine what the actions are that prove the family or individuals within the family are living each guiding principle. This is how a family can measure their emotional growth and how well the guiding principles are working, or as we like to call it, "becoming and embodying the learning," meaning being governance in action by doing different than past negative emotional traditions would have us do.

Here are examples of guiding principles I have seen families develop in doing this work together:

Guiding Principle = Acceptance

What does acceptance look like?

- Trust.
- Support.
- Respect.
- Appreciating differences.

What is the behavior that creates acceptance?

- We listen to each other.
- We are open-minded.
- We seek to understand.

The actions to live *acceptance* are curiosity and active listening

Guiding Principle = Transparency

What does transparency look like?

- Openness and honesty with each other
- Forthcoming.

» Truthful.
» Feeling free to speak one's mind.

What is the behavior that creates transparency?

» Not hiding.
» Not lying.

The action to live *transparency* is speak the truth

The Path to Vision, Mission & Purpose

What is your *why*, your purpose? That is a big question to ask yourself and to ponder. For a family it is an even bigger one. For many families, regardless of resources, wealth is a factor in determining the family's mission. I see a family's wealth as being made up of three distinct and unique components:

Family Wealth = Financial Capital +
Human Capital + Social Capital.

Financial Capital are the material assets that belong to the family; the business, the real estate portfolio, the stocks, bonds, and private equity portfolios, the art, the wine, the things.

Human Capital is the individuals who make up the family—and their emotions.

Social Capital is the collection of individuals plus their collective social standing and reputation.

If a family is to determine their family purpose, vision, and mission, it has to be based on the entire family wealth, not just the financial component. The collective purpose has to be lived by the individuals as does the vision and mission. There must be buy-in from an emotional perspective for these to have any strong foundation and lasting impact, or legacy. That buy-in comes from the individual emotional wealth of all members of that family. These are the foundations of how a family designs their emotional legacy by living and embodying their purpose, vision, and mission.

For example, here is how one family we worked with identified their purpose, vision and mission:

Family Vision: What we want to achieve.
Transformation.
Family Mission: How we execute the purpose.
Transparency through vulnerability.
Family Purpose: Why.
To empower for community impact.

For many families, establishing a new purpose, vision and mission requires letting go of the old one they inherited. Accepting an ending and letting go of the why that was attached to the old negative emotional traditions of the family is a deeply emotional process that will bring up fear, grief and resistance. It can be reframed into an act of continuity, trust, and transformation. Human emotions—individually and collectively—are assets as vital as the material resources of the family or group. The emotional traditions designed through this process establish the family or group as a dynasty formed around a set of guiding principles. In our process of family meetings, there are a few framing concepts parents and leaders should consider in order to understand how their family or group could function as a dynasty:

1. **Legacy.** Your family exhibits an expression of values that have been embedded into its structure. Understanding what these values are, and why they are worth preserving is important to communicate. Dynasty-minded families practice ethical foresight in that they see themselves as stewards of an emotional legacy. As part of this process, parents and children (or in groups, leaders and successors) cooperatively develop **Emotional Governance Pathways**—systems to regulate the inevitable human emotions that show up in the family dynamics and communicate about them. They define and establish a new set of **Guiding Principles**—the standards, rules, responsibilities and roles they will operate within, and the consequences of crossing those boundaries.

2. **Continuity.** A dynasty-minded family cultivates continuity; it's in how you communicate, how you manage emotions, how you make decisions, and especially in how you solve problems and meet challenges. Parents and children building preparedness are perfectly positioned to explore what continuity means to the family by identifying the touchstones of the family's continuity, which are worth preserving and which could be evolved by the succession of children into their adult autonomy.

3. **Adaptation.** Dynasties do not endure by freezing the past—if they do, they don't last longer than external circumstances allow them to. Knowing where your family can remain *principled* while remaining *flexible* can help you

avoid the trap of operating from the Three Assumptions. In the family meetings, parents and children define what their new emotional traditions will be and look like, within the family. They also define the parameters and qualifications; there can be no ambiguity around what this looks like.

4. **Dynasty.** Lastly, they assemble every understanding they have accumulated from the steps in the process into a statement capturing a vision, mission, and purpose. The statement connects to the family's emotional wealth, not just the material or resources wealth of the family.

The path is to continuously move from ambiguity to clarity around every value, every role and every principle. This process is scalable. It has to start by each participating individual before it can be accomplished by the group.

Defining your family's dynasty using these concepts might help you understand what in the family's emotional legacy is worth preserving and what might be worth letting go, trusting the next generation to *add* to the continuity of the family as a dynasty. The ending of one dynasty and the rise of another has been, through our humanity, a cycle of upheaval full of great trials. Every dynasty embodies its own unique mythology: of origins, of rights, of purpose, of destiny. The structures of emotion that live within them, embodied in the hearts and minds of all those who keep the dynasty alive will need reorientation. That is the opportunity of succession, to be the mechanism that allows a dynasty—and all it represents—to adapt to the future and to endure.

Questions to ponder:

1. In what ways does your family dynasty reflect your personal values, identity, or family history?

2. How might those values evolve or endure?

3. If your emotional traditions were to outlive you, what kind of social, ethical, or cultural impact would you want them to have on your community over the next 100 years?

4. What unspoken emotional traditions already exist within your family or group dynamic that could serve as the foundation of a "dynastic identity" for later generations ?

5. How do you envision the emotional experience of letting go—entrusting your life's work to someone else?

6. What would need to be in place for that to feel like continuity rather than loss?

7. What balance would you want your children or successors to achieve between preserving what you built and adapting it to their own era?

8. What emotional inheritance do you want your children or successors to receive from your legacy?

CHAPTER 14

The Boy Scout & the Ferrari

In 1908, Robert Baden-Powell published *Scouting for Boys*, the blueprint for the Boy Scouts. Rising to the status of national hero in Britain, Baden-Powell had been a Colonel in the British Army during the Boer War in South Africa. During the Siege of Mafeking—where 1,500 defenders held off an attacking force of 8,000 Boers—the Dutch-speaking colonists of South Africa. Baden-Powell had been awestruck by the resourcefulness, and calm under pressure exhibited by Mafeking's defenders. "Be Prepared means you are always in a state of readiness in mind and body to do your duty," he wrote in *Scouting for Boys*. For Baden-Powell Preparedness meant Intellectual readiness: Learning skills ahead of time—not just memorizing facts but practicing how to act. Physical readiness: Being trained and fit enough to act, from being ready to help someone in need to surviving a crisis. And moral readiness: Being prepared to do the right thing, always—even when it's hard.

The book was an immediate sensation and gave rise to an institution for learning and personal development through the great outdoors. The Boy Scouts use the motto "Be Prepared" to encourage readiness in mind and body to act in any situation—whether it is a challenge, natural disaster, emergency or opportunity to help others. An individual Boy Scout is in themselves a packed and ready survival bag with every tool inside: knowledge, character, fitness, and hands-on skills, ready to meet any unpredictable situation effectively with emotional calm and a code of ethics to guide them.

Imagine this: You have a child who has just become old enough to legally drive. You have abundant resources, and you have enrolled them at the best driving school, and they have earned their permit. You want them to enjoy the freedom of coming and going as they please and no longer depending on you to play chauffeur. You want to gift them their first car and you want to create an experience for them. You could buy them a Kia with four cylinders and not too much power until they learn to be responsible on the road. But a part of you, possibly now that you've built wealth, wants them to have something special, maybe something you never had when you were their age.

You decide to surprise them with a Ferrari. But, before they are allowed to take it for a spin, you bring them to the Ferrari factory in Italy and introduce them to the people who work there. Only the people who design and build these beautiful precision cars with their own hands have the facility to teach your child about what it means to own a Ferrari.

Your child meets with the head designer to learn about the aerodynamics and the engine nuances of the car, the chief mechanic to understand how the car functions and how to maintain it, and the CFO to gain a grasp of the financial margins each car contributes to the bottom line of the company. Finally your child meets with the current CEO who shares the history of the company, the emotional traditions that won Ferrari years of dominance on the track at Le Mans, and the company's vision for the future.

Now your child knows Ferrari. Equipped with a wealth of knowledge about the car, they gleefully return home ready to take it out and, "See what this baby can do!" Excited, you hop-in with them, trusting that with the best driving instruction money can buy and a trip to Italy to learn about owning a Ferrari from the craftsmen that make them, they are set up for the drive and that you're both in capable hands. The engine starts, and you both set off for your first ride together in the new gift.

As your child approaches the open road, a freeway or a four-lane coastal road with a wide sweep of easy, drifting curves, they say, "Let's open her up and let her run." Your child shifts gears and lays on the gas, you both feel the press into the seatbacks as the strength of 812 horses under the hood.

The next thing you know, both of you are waking up in hospital beds. Slowly it all comes back to you, foggy at first. The car leaping forward, both of you yawping a "Ya–hoo!" as you are caught up in the exhilaration of what feels like an unlimited source of humming, surging power. And, caught up in the feeling of it all, your child loses sight of the road for a brief millisecond.

How could this possibly have happened? You sent your child to get an "education" about the car. They learned about the working of the car, the financial side, the history and vision of the company—all great and useful Intellectual knowledge. And yet, they were still unprepared to handle the *authentic* car on the *actual* road in *real* dynamic driving conditions where the only thing that can be expected is the unexpected. What was missing in their preparedness?

First, let's define preparedness as the quality or state of readiness, or preparation. Preparedness involves four components:

- **Intellectual Preparedness**—the what and the how of responsibility
- **Practical Preparedness**—the knowledge, skills and technical understanding needed to perform the tasks; how to respond to changing, unpredictable conditions, and how to handle the effects associated with power
- **Experiential Preparedness**—hands-on knowledge
- **Emotional preparedness**—how to handle the feelings that arise when pushing yourself or your organization to maximum performance; the state of awareness necessary to not allow yourself to lose focus on the terrains, conditions ahead, and destination; knowing what guardrails are in place to keep the car on the road

All are concurrently necessary. Driving a Ferrari and having responsibility and power in adult life have a similar set of risks in that we can easily become lost in the immense power of the experience, and we might take our eyes off of the road long enough to end up in a detour or a crash.

Peter, one of my Veritage clients, was the oldest of three siblings. From the outside, he seemed to have everything together; he was well-educated, responsible, and a natural leader. Yet inside, he struggled with quiet but constant self-doubt. No matter how much he achieved, he found it excruciating to trust his own decisions.

In coaching, Peter began to uncover more and more about where this lack of self-trust came from. Growing up, he felt overshadowed by his two younger siblings who excelled in sports. In Peter's family, success was measured on the playing field, and his father—stoic and focused on peak performance—placed little emphasis on emotional connection. Young Peter, not as athletic as his siblings, sought his father's approval in the only way he knew how: by excelling in academics. He stacked up achievements, degrees, and credentials, hoping each new success would finally win the recognition he craved. His false equation was Achievement = Approval = Safety.

But Peter's father's approval never seemed to come in the way he craved. Instead, he absorbed a negative emotional tradition that said, "Feelings weren't safe to have—let alone express." Over time, this left him increasingly emotionally disconnected from himself and from his siblings. He developed a punishing inner voice that constantly berated him, telling him he wasn't good enough and should already "know all the answers." When he inevitably didn't, he turned that disappointment inward, feeding a cycle of self-criticism.

The breakthrough came when Peter saw this pattern clearly. He realized that the harshness he directed at himself was also causing collateral damage in his relationships, like debris from a car crash injuring bystanders—especially with his siblings. In that moment, he began to recognize his right to feel—to be human, not just a performer. Peter softened toward the little boy inside him, a little boy who had grown up denied emotional safety and bereft of acceptance and he shifted his internal reality from being dictated by his own harshest judge to becoming a source of compassion for himself and others.

What Peter had been missing all along wasn't more achievements—it was emotional preparedness, the ability to accept and allow his feelings. That shift transformed his relationships. Instead of leading through pressure and expectation, he began leading with empathy, showing by example that strength includes vulnerability. In reclaiming his right to feel without judgment or shame Peter became emotionally prepared to face life with resilience and connection.

In my work with families, there are some interesting findings that I see as repeatable emotional traditions which lead to parents putting their children into the metaphorical Ferrari unprepared.

For many the succession to full autonomy can be paralyzing, If the results are bad, we get blamed. Trust is broken, doubt sets in and people begin to chime in with negativity and judgement—*if it wasn't for their mother/father, they would never have had a chance to be in this position in the first place.* On the other hand, if the results are good, they might be called The Entitled Brat, being served an unearned prosperity on a silver spoon.

For some next generations, these circumstances could feel like a *Kobayashi Maru* test—an iconic test from the television and film franchise, *Star Trek*, where a simulated scenario only ever leads to a bad outcome. In the test a Starfleet cadet, training to one day become the Captain of a starship, commands their simulated ship from a simulated bridge, the command center of the ship, surrounded by other cadets who might be friends or even rivals. Their ship is operating on the edge of the Neutral Zone—a political boundary established by treaty after a brutal interstellar war between Earth's Starfleet and the warlike Klingon Empire. If a ship from either side crosses into the Neutral Zone, that action violates the treaty and the war resumes.

Inevitably, the cadet's ship receives a distress call. A commercial freighter named the *Kobayashi Maru* claims to have struck a mine, lost power, drifted into the Neutral Zone and is under heavy attack by a pair of deadly Klingon Cruisers. Alarmingly, the message is audio only. The cadet and their crew hear the desperate pleas of civilians in danger. The cadet then has a decision to make: Assume the distress call is genuine and cross into the Neutral Zone to rescue the freighter, violating the treaty, or assume the distress call is actually a Klingon Trap meant to bait the cadet's ship into crossing the Neutral Zone. If they do that, they potentially leave the *Kobayashi maru* to a grim fate, the alternative being they cross into the Neutral Zone to rescue the *Kobayashi Maru* only to be ambushed and destroyed by the overwhelming brutality of a wing of Klingon ships. The test is in actuality one of character; how a Starfleet Captain in training emotionally faces the inevitability of defeat, death, loss or failure.

The *Kobayashi Maru* test in *Star Trek* is a tool for emotional preparedness. It communicates to the person-in-learning, "The unexpected is part of this business of life, and failure is part of it too. And it's important for you to know who you are when those circumstances arise—because they will arise. Regardless of how prepared you are practically, you also need to emotionally prepare for this reality."

The typical pattern of behavior for parents, one I have seen over and over again, is to mystify adulthood by keeping their children at arm's length while they are young. The key to emotionally preparing the next generation is to include them in the emotional dynamics of the family from the beginning. If the time for that has already passed, then the next best thing may be to include them in the emotional dynamics of the family now and doing so with the tools of a Safe Space established to deal with the inevitable dust the rising emotions will kick up.

Parents in this process need to understand three things:

1. How will this affect their familial relationships and conversations in the future?

2. What should they do in response?

3. And most importantly, how can they open up about their feelings around all of it?

The Process Shift of Trust

Why is the transition into autonomy such an emotional time? Beyond the feelings that are emerging throughout the process and the familial patterns and emotional traditions that are being talked about—maybe even deconstructed for the first time—shifts in the way the family is functioning emotionally are occurring. Things will be different than the way they were before and that requires a two-way trust: Trust from the parent that the children have the full spectrum of preparedness to meet the demands of life—especially emotional preparedness. And trust from the children in their own abilities and their own decision-making.

A model for building that trust should include a **shared narrative**—the "who we are and what brought us here," piece that focuses on storytelling and the emotional understanding, not the mythology that has upheld the family's negative emotional traditions. Parents can share what the legacy means to them in terms of values, vision or the sacrifices they have made to build it. Children then can share their hopes and goals for the future of that legacy. Next it should include a **value alignment**—the "what matters to each of us and how do we collaborate" piece. Parents and children work together to define who decides the non-negotiable emotional traditions (more often parents), what is flexible in the new emotional tradition (collaborative).

Lastly, the process should include a **feedback system**, a way for both generations to check-in using their Safe Space to examine what's working, what feels uncertain and what needs to shift. Without a structured process of transitioning the emotional traditions within a family that includes the feelings of all members, the past and the emotions associated with it will show up and bring the unexpected; if the older brother stole the younger brother's girlfriend when they were teenagers, the younger might not trust the older to make the big family decisions. He might likely exclude him altogether.

Whenever there is a human social group—whether a family or an organization, trust, respect and inclusion are necessary when making decisions. Getting into a Safe Space with structured dialog and having the difficult and awkward conversations gets some of the unexpected emotional hazards on the road where they can be seen and responded to ahead of time, before there can be a high-speed crash, because no matter what you are driving, you're part of the car.

Questions to ponder:

1. How are you intellectually prepared to carry on your family's legacy?

2. How are you practically prepared to take on your family's legacy?

3. How are you experientially prepared to take on your family's legacy?

4. How are you emotionally prepared to take on your family's legacy?

CHAPTER 15

Fine Tuning

Every human being has to contend with their own emotional DNA. This is an incredibly difficult and challenging enterprise in and of itself. Children, as they grow into adults, and members of the next generation face a specific set of challenges as they cultivate preparedness to take on the responsibility of their inherited autonomy. They are not only transitioning into a new role relative to the established emotional dynasty of the family or group, with its own values and ways of doing things, but they are also bringing forth their own set of values and visions that will inevitably have an effect on the dynasty. The next generation needs to think of their succession into autonomy or leadership in any area of life as an emotional dynasty.

You design your future in relationships, in achievement, in life. Fine tuning is about *how* you show up in that designed future.

The sport of Rugby is called by its devotees "a hooligan's game played by gentlemen." It is a kinetic mélange of beauty and brutality played on nearly every continent on Earth. The break, the moment the ball enters play, happens like a gasp in a cathedral. Spinning end-over-end like a thrown secret through a fissure of sound and hunger, the ball slips free of the maul of scrambling players—and it's snatched. Now the Winger is prey, hands clawing air too slow to stop him. He's not running; he's been flung—forward, through time, through memory, through every backyard dream stitched into his black jersey threads. The line's there—painted, mythic. He dives. The moment stretches like a held note before a chorus. More points, yes—but more than that, a reckoning. A whisper into the void that says: We were here.

Rugby can trace its origins to 1823, where, at Rugby School in Warwickshire in Great Britain, William Webb Ellis savagely violated the rules of football (soccer) by picking up the ball and running with it during a match. Although the legend of Ellis's transgressive realignment as a true historical story is much debated by Rugby fans, it lets us in on the adaptive and rebellious essence at the heart of the game. By the twentieth century Rugby had caught on throughout Great Britain and the Empire, especially in Wales, South Africa, Australia and New Zealand.

Before humans arrived there, New Zealand was a land teeming with birds. These South Pacific islands have only been inhabited for around 850 years. Some of the last land in the world ever settled by humans, the first Polynesians arrived by canoe on New Zealand in the late 1200s. Because of its unique geography and climate of lower temperatures, deep forests and seasons, these Polynesian settlers—coming from the hotter more tropical climates of the Mid-Pacific—would have to align and adapt to New Zealand

Over several generations, as they settled the land, these Polynesians formed a distinct tribal outgrowth with its own dialect, mythology and customs: the Māori. First, they connected a spiritual and genealogical tie to the land; each Māori group or *iwi* would begin to trace its dynasty from a specific *waka* or canoe that had landed there. They attached deep spiritual significance to every mountain, stream or valley they settled—the land became part of their identity.

In 1768 English sea Captain James Cook became the first European to have contact with the Māori tribes of New Zealand. This first contact with strange and alien people was peaceful, based on trade and mutual cooperation. By 1840, Great Britain and the Māori had signed the Treaty of Waitangi, all but guaranteeing the Island nation's status as a British colony by 1841. A series of bloody wars of possession between the Māori and the British would ensue and by 1877, the Māori, weary of war, and faced with an unending tide of British colonists, were forced to assimilate.

Perhaps one of the most recognizable cultural symbols of the Māori, known throughout the globe as the signature tradition of New Zealand, is the *haka*—a traditional "posture dance" used as a performative ritual to unify the Māori people and express a sacred emotion. Traditionally, the haka were performed to welcome guests, honor the ancestors, celebrate victories, mourn the dead, or challenge rivals. The haka comes down through Māori mythology; the luminescent god Tāne-rore who the Māori believed embodied the shimmering heat of Summer and channeled it into a life-force that could be harnessed and projected.

The haka does not begin with sound. It begins with breath—tight in the chest, a storm coiling in the gut. Hands slap thighs like war drums—channeling spiritual power, a lightning strike in the form of a man. It is the emotive force of a people's ancestors bellowed as an incantation, a declaration of intent.

The haka became a global phenomenon in the early twentieth century, a gift of Rugby. New Zealand rugby teams touring the British Empire were known to perform the haka as a pre-match ritual since 1884. Today, the All Blacks, New Zealand's national rugby union team perform the haka as a pre-match ritual to packed stadiums and a global audience of millions, making the haka a globally recognized and iconic symbol of New Zealand's identity, heritage and evocative force.

Today, the All Blacks, are considered by rugby fans all over the world as one of the most iconic and superior franchises regardless of the sport. For the 125 years of their existence, they have created a cohesive identity—an emotional dynasty—that transcends oceans, national borders, and languages. Everyone, whether they are rugby fans or not, knows the All Blacks and definitely knows the haka.

The All Blacks didn't gain their legendary reputation by luck or by a few explosive bursts of winning as a team. The team built their legacy with consistency of performance, year after year, decade after decade, generation after generation. Many great players in the All Blacks have come and gone. Yet the All Blacks have retained something unique and irreplaceable but not irreplicable: a modern mythology as one of the greatest franchises in any sport in the world.

Human nature is highly adaptive. That adaptability is part of what's allowed us to survive in the harshest of conditions on Earth, but adaptability can be a liability in how it can enable us to adapt to conditions and patterns that perhaps don't serve our best interests. During any period of constant victory, it's easy to become comfortable. Consistent victory without adversity or the occasional failure usually doesn't teach us much unless we are actively designing a mindset of constant learning and constant improvement.

During those many years of winning, the All Blacks had a readiness discipline embodied in their practice of always studying what worked in a match and what didn't. Over time, they learned exactly which strategies carved a path to victory, they honed those strategies into a set of core guiding principles in order to maintain their success in the sport and their cohesion as a team.

Leave the Jersey in a Better Place

According to James Kerr's seminal book, *Legacy: What The All Blacks Can Teach Us About The Business Of Life*, there are 15 guiding principles that form the emotional legacy of the All Blacks. I want to focus on one, "Leaving the jersey in a better place." In other words, any player on the All Blacks must be aware, at all times no matter the circumstances, or conditions, that he will not be wearing his jersey forever. Whether by time, or choice, or circumstance, he *will* be replaced at some point.

Moving through the world with this knowledge deeply internalized gives each All Blacks player the opportunity to make their contribution to the team count, and to transition out of that legacy leaving it better than where it was when they came into it, by virtue of their contribution. When you retire, you must want to leave your jersey in a better place for those who come after you.

When we sit with that for a moment and think of the confidence this gives the incoming player. The All Blacks are giving them a pathway to meet one of their biggest challenges. A massive and integral part of human identity revolves around being part of the tribe or the group. Whether a tribe on the African Savannah, a company, a rock band, or a sports team being a contributor to the group, one who makes their mark on the effort, and who leaves a lasting legacy behind them, is an important motivator for all human beings. Being offered this emotional tradition of leaving the jersey in a better place by the person who filled the jersey before them could give the Next Generation that head-start. What they do from there is up to them. But they know one thing to be true: their job will be to leave the jersey in a better place than where they found it on their first day. Leaving the jersey in a better place is an emotional tradition that helps keep them on the right path.

How might leaving the jersey in a better place translate to the emotional dynamics of families and groups? The first step is an internal step. It's about your mindset and about how **you must see the positive emotional legacy you have designed in your life as a foundational element of the dynasty that will outlast you.**

Whether by choice, time, or circumstances, your stewardship of that emotional legacy will come to an end and it will transition to the next generation or those who succeed you. Just as any player in the All Blacks knows and accepts that the jersey will outlast them, all members of families and groups must make peace with the fact that the emotional legacy will outlast them and turn that difficult to accept fact into an opportunity.

A parent or visionary leader of a group might have a difficult time handing over their jersey to the next player: their child(ren) or successors. So, they do what human beings have done for millions of years, they fight and pull against the inevitable; they do everything in their power to keep the jersey in their hands. And they lose it anyway.

Rigidity against change is not what makes a great dynasty—practically or emotionally— and it isn't what will create generational wealth that sustains within a family. Anyone with the impostor mindset that says, "I built this, and without me there will be nothing," is only a player in the game, creating a role for themselves. While that solves a fundamental human problem of resources and survival, there is no legacy in that future because they aren't focused on the longevity of the business beyond the needs of the impostor, and they aren't building the emotional future that will enable their emotional legacy to survive and outlast them.

To shift away from the impostor's rigidity and move towards the emotional willingness necessary to transition an emotional tradition operating within a family or a group, the second step is to **internalize the awareness that there cannot be an end goal in the group—the group will always be evolving over time** and a group that makes dynastic longevity one of its core values, focused on leaving the jersey in a better place, ensures the future and has governance in place that can help the group design that future state. Families don't have finish lines. **Any group with a constructive emotional legacy will be managed differently than any focused only on short-term goals.**

Building the Confidence to Set New Traditions

For the All Blacks, Saturday is game day, a day of intense focus and immense will built on a foundation of preparedness. Each of the players knows the intensity he is expected to bring to the game. The rugby pitch is, for the All Blacks, the modern equivalent of a sacred space; intensity, focus and willpower must be harnessed and brought to the pitch again-and-again, replicated. This is the second function of the haka. It makes the setting of intention and the willingness of both a player's mind and body into a repertoire of honed actions that have been burned into the cells by constant practice.

The same intensity we see in a game must also exist on the practice field during the week leading up to each game. Most rugby teams that play on Saturdays take a light week. They practice with a repertoire of tactics and strategies in mind and let their bodies rest for the game. They are investing in recovered and rested bodies to command the field. The All Blacks are different. When their players step onto the practice field on Thursdays, they play with the exact same level and degree of game day intensity; they prepare for the maul by putting themselves into the simulation. This guiding principle, called "Train to Win" uses practice under pressure, simulating match-day intensity, to build resilience.

This wasn't always the case for the All Blacks. It took a major defeat during a critical season to spark the change. Rugby legend Anton Oliver made the New Zealand All Blacks rugby team at a Bledisloe cup test match in 1995 when he was a rare and young 19 years old, "I was big for my age" as Anton explained nostalgically. At 1.84 Meters tall and 111 Kgs (6' and 244 lbs.), his size gave him the edge he needed to claim his place on the venerable team, and he never looked back.

His father, Frank Oliver, had been an All Blacks Captain, commanding the team in four matches from 1976 to 1981, playing the position of the Lock—often the tallest man on a rugby team and the source of much of its physical power. Often referred to as 'the engine room' by rugby fans, a Lock must have the ability to secure the ball and use explosive running force to power through the forceful contact of other players.

Anton's All Blacks career lasted for 10 years, from 1997 to 2007, ending in a year considered by many All Blacks fans to be a tumultuous one that saw five different coaches come-and-go. For Anton, the

All Blacks manager—regardless of who is at the helm—is in effect much like a CEO or other visionary leader. Each time a new person steps into the role, they get rid of all the old supporting staff, bring in people with whom they've worked with and trust, and they bring in their own personality, vision for the team and approach. Every iteration could be jarring to players who have been working together for months or years. Suddenly, a new coach or manager shows up and does everything in their power to exorcise the last person's legacy.

In 125 years of rugby union history, the All Blacks are the highest-winning franchise. The pressures on them to perform are immense. The legacy they embody and uphold is a demanding one. This is no different than a family or a group with a long entrenched emotional legacy. Venerable organizations have a lot to prove and when major adjustments like changes in leadership inevitably occur, it could cause panic.

For Anton, with the end of the 2002 Super 12 club rugby season in sight, he had captained the All Blacks for one year, when the unexpected happened. He ruptured his Achilles' tendon, an injury that would cost him his entire 2003 season. Almost as quickly as the captaincy came it was gone. A new captain took his place. When Anton healed and regained a position on the team, the All Blacks stayed with the new captain. Anton could have been devastated by this decision, but he was doing different in that, he had been working on a set of guiding principles that he brought into how he showed up for the All Blacks when he wore the jersey; guiding principles such as, "Play with Purpose–Ask 'Why?'—align individual goals with team purpose; purpose fuels performance" and "No D__kheads"–character over talent. Ego disrupts culture; humility strengthens it."

Anton embraced the team's decision. Far more than wanting to be captain again, Anton had asked himself how he could be supportive.

Navigating his position as once again a regular player whereas before he had been the team's captain, initially presented significant awkwardness. Yet, over time, Anton designed a new role for himself: the new captain's "big brother." He recognized it was the "little brother's" turn to take over and lead. Designing this new role was how he could meaningfully help the team and just as importantly define a new sense of purpose for himself.

Having the Courage to face an old Tradition

In 2007, the All Blacks faced France in the World Cup quarterfinals. The eyes of the world were fixed on this match and tensions were high. The legacy of both teams, two of the best in the sport, was on the line. The All Blacks were favored to carry the day and had been carrying a reassuring lead at halftime but Murphy's Law—what can happen, will happen—intervened and, in a shocking turn of events, despite their rigorous training, and mental discipline, the All Blacks were defeated. The unexpected French win upset the expectations of rugby fans all over the world.

When the All Blacks lost this World Cup quarterfinals to France in 2007, they panicked. They hadn't been emotionally prepared for a loss. *What had gone wrong*, Anton would think to himself as the All Blacks internalized the outcome and regrouped for the next season. Anton went into analysis mode, deconstructing what had caused the loss and he realized that the Emotional Tradition of a minority of players on the All Blacks had spread throughout the team, like a virus of the mind: the fear of failure.

The specter of failure was showing up in how the All Blacks trained. The team had lost tempo. It was taking them 20 minutes to get warmed up on the field to reach game speed. When they looked at their training week, they had spent 56 hours without any kind of intensity. Anton's response was to encourage a stepping up of their tempo during the All Blacks' practices; redouble their confidence on the pitch and play with twice the intensity that would be expected in a game. Bringing that energy to their Thursday practice, 48 hours before game day, became a new emotional tradition: "Fail Fast, Learn Faster." Continuous improvement is the key to growth, so when in doubt create a collective learning environment.

The pressure was on. The century-old team had brought their all and performed well the next season. There was no room for error, not even during the transition. The traditions of the team—positive or negative would stick with them. For the All Blacks, their negative tradition had been *the players must perform*, which is very similar to the pressure children and successors can feel as they grow closer to a time when they gain the responsibility of full autonomy. In groups, human beings push themselves to live up to a standard and an old tradition that they didn't necessarily create. For example, many members of families feel they don't have the agency to modify or evolve a standing emotional tradition in the family; as if to do so would somehow corrupt the family's legacy. However, conditions change and in order to survive and thrive in changing conditions, we have to adapt, or we perish. It is a law of nature.

Families often reinforce an idealized archetype—an original model or type after which other similar things are patterned—for every role within the family. Without these archetypes the family likely wouldn't survive the harsh conditions of the environment. Groups extend these dynamics beyond the family, adapting their own emotional traditions and scaling the archetypes that maintain them to the level of the organization, the community, and even the nation. There had existed an archetypal blueprint of who an All Black player should be. It was based on a post-World War II model: White, married, farmer-stock type of man who is stoic, never expresses his emotions, who simply like a wrecking-ball smashes the other guy and carries the ball to a win. More machine than man, anything outside that mold, it was assumed, wouldn't serve the team and therefore wasn't allowed.

The All Blacks had a legacy problem; They were still viewing themselves as the same group of brutes that made the team famous a century before. The idealized archetype that had maintained the way the All Blacks functioned in an earlier time with different pressures and different conditions—was holding them back from victory. Changing external conditions demand changing emotional traditions. New Zealand's immigration policy opened up in the 1970s, the population became far more diverse, and it quickly became apparent that, in order for the All Blacks to gain the most effective players, the emotional model they lived by needed to evolve too.

However, when facing France in 2007, instead of feeling empowered by their legacy, they imploded under the weight of it, and the All Black's captain realized that a singular feeling held in common among the team was lying in wait at the root of their failure: It wasn't fun being an All Black anymore. The All Blacks were stuck in a tradition of silence. They were not talking about how they felt, and the silence crushed their potential under an unspoken fear of making mistakes. Had they created a structured dialogue—a Safe

Space—sooner, they would have likely realized they were all feeling that fear of failure. They had blindly tried to uphold that tradition of emotional silence but when they were defeated by France and felt the weight of their legacy pressing down on them, they knew they needed to do different. They knew they needed to change *something*.

After some digging, they knew what they needed: vulnerability. Having that feeling out in the open where it can be in consensus, felt together, it can be realized and transformed into fuel. The All Blacks needed to reconceptualize their relationship to their legacy, just like families have to do. They had to design collectively a vision of walking towards the pressure. Each player individually had to accept, acknowledge, and embrace the thing that they were afraid of. "You could see the team transform," Anton later recalled. The bigger the pressure, the better and faster they played. They immediately won several games, in the bare last five minutes of play, that by rights they never should have won.

The All Blacks had rebuilt themselves individually and unified collectively under a new emotional tradition of breaking the wall of silence and running towards the fear, and it had brought them into a place where they knew they were going to win, even when they shouldn't. It didn't matter who was wearing the opposing jersey—**the All Blacks were competing against themselves**. They were improving from the inside and playing each as a chance to prove to themselves how much their mindset had improved.

The All Blacks collectively realized that the team would exist beyond each one of them individually. Eventually, whether by injury, age, time or conditions, new players would emerge to take their place. In this awareness, they were to design their future with longevity in mind—knowing the team's legacy, positive or negative, would outlast them. So, why not make it a positive one and leave the jersey in a better place? The All Blacks would mark this journey through their vulnerability by creating a new Haka as part of their process of transformation.

Like all great athletes, most human beings want to succeed as well as contribute. They want to compete at a level that honors the past and the legacy they carry. And more importantly, the next generation has the support of a parent or leader who is prepared to leave the jersey in a better place. You must view your dynasty as something that will outlast you and live by that understanding.

That's the hallmark of a great emotional succession plan in life.

Having the Courage to Set a New Tradition

The team that was known for 125 years as the team of emotionless machines who ran out onto the field and smashed people around had now admitted that they needed emotional help—they identified their white elephant. Each player was going on his personal ascent, allowing all of them to remove themselves from the Land of Familiar. Through structured dialogue, they learned to trust themselves and each other in the face of fear and took a risk; one which the team's existing leadership would have never approved of, because it wasn't *their* way of doing things.

The old version of the All Blacks would have reacted to the fear by training harder. Getting angrier. Putting more work in the weight room and releasing any players who weren't willing to put their bodies on the line for a win. But the new generation of All Blacks responded to the fear by taking a different path. And it was one that would transform the team back to its winning ways.

In 2011, the All Blacks again faced France, this time in the World Cup finals, and they won by a single point. They have remained in the winning column ever since and still defend their title as the most successful international men's rugby team of all time, with a staggering winning percentage of over 77 percent since 1903. Anton Oliver left the All Blacks after the 2007 team. He wasn't able to be on the field for their 2011 win against France. But he and the players who donned the jersey just a few short years prior had changed the course of a franchise that had been on the brink of struggle for the first time in its century-old existence; and they did that by taking a giant leap of faith, believing in themselves, and creating a new tradition for a new generation of rugby players and fans of the game from all over the world.

Whether in sports, in work or in life, a crucial tool for adaptation to the flux of external circumstances is to **respond, not react, to what arises.** When we react to a challenge or a difficult situation we are allowing our Sympathetic Nervous System to dictate our thoughts and actions. This can cause damage to whatever we care about and are trying to protect—a sports team, the legacy of a business, the relational bonds of a family. When we respond, we allow the emotional and somatic shock we feel from our nervous system to happen, and we also allow a pause; a moment of consideration before we communicate or make a decision. Cultivating this discipline is what helped Anton Oliver realize why the All Blacks had failed and why they needed to reshape the traditions of the team. When you respond to your perception instead of reacting to it, you can do different. This can be as simple as putting on a crisp clean shirt and shaving before you do any of the important tasks of the day, even if you're at home and no one would see you.

The most important thing to do, when you decide to act and face old emotional traditions to design new ones, is to ask, "what would my Safe Space do in this situation?" If your Safe Space is connection, then what *reaction* might interfere with building connection and what *response* might act in service of building connection? By ritualizing a shift in your mindset that says, *when I do X, I show up as Y* and making that into a constant discipline is how you fine tune your legacy and shape everything you have influence over, especially the emotional dynasty of your business, and the emotional traditions of your family. No matter our resources, your socioeconomic background, or your exact circumstances, this discipline costs nothing except for the milliseconds it takes for the signals that fire in your nervous system, the ones that are urging you to react with big, intense emotions—upset, anger, rage, frustration, sadness, fear—whatever they happen to be, and harness them into something that is intentional and might create the kind of alignment with others that means the difference between failure and success, leadership and ownership of the emotional legacy. What is your family legacy? What will outlast you? Who will wear your jersey after you, and how can you leave it in a better place for them?

Questions to ponder:

1. How can you take a lesson from the All Blacks playbook and leave the jersey in a better place than you found it, in your family?

2. What are the traditions of your family that are positive and worthy of preservation?

3. How are those traditions operating within your family and how are they serving you?

4. What are some of the old traditions you must confront in your family?

5. What new traditions might you create to evolve the old traditions that are holding you captive?

CHAPTER 16

Futurist

The ascent is one of the most challenging and important undertakings any human being can choose. It is one way to, as Anton Oliver did for the All Blacks, walk towards the pressure; to have the confidence to face old traditions and design new ones. You might be asking, "Okay, I've climbed out of the Land of Familiar and made it to the summit. Now what?"

First, take a moment to appreciate where you are. Appreciate the view from the summit and the perspective it has given you on the landscape and yourself. Look back on the arduous emotional climb you just completed and then celebrate gaining the summit with those who tackled summiting alongside you, who braved the ropes of difficult and awkward conversations and who anchored you by showing up in all their vulnerability to co-create the Safe Space with you. It's easy to forget to celebrate our wins yet it's important, as my friend Artist and Futurist Jamie Mustard calls it, "to stamp your passport."

What he means by stamping your passport is to have a ritual with the people who are there, walking the challenging paths with you: go to dinner together, break bread together, talk about the experience you've just had together, and mark the moment. It is important to acknowledge and celebrate every victory, not to hit every milestone and keep going without a pause. This kind of ritual anchors the work you do in deep meaning, and it makes building and creating with others, about community not just teamwork. This ritual of stamping the passport is the groundwork for what will become not only the answer to the question, "Now what?" It will also be part of the work that comes next: Maintaining the summit.

Most people, when they imagine climbing a mountain, think getting to the summit is the goal, that the danger stops there; that there will be no more challenges after reaching the summit. They imagine enjoying the view from the mountain's peak, taking selfies, and facing no danger on the trek home. But gaining the summit is not the goal. Being on the summit and holding your ground there against the dizzying heights, the low oxygen, the biting and unpredictable winds and eventually making a safe transit off the mountain is the goal. "It is one thing to decide to climb a mountain. It is quite another to be on top of it." Those words, credited to Herbert A. Simon, an American Decision Making Expert and cognitive scholar who developed the science of "satisficing"—a method for decision making based on pushing the minimal standard of what is acceptable—illustrate what so many of us often forget. On the summit, you must operate differently than you did when you were far below, on the valley floor in the Land of Familiar. A different set of skills and different alignment with the conditions of the summit is necessary to keep your position on the summit a stable one.

A portmanteau of "satisfying" and "sufficing" and presented to the world of sciences in 1956, satisficing works by using a process of elimination to choose a course of action based on a minimum standard threshold of acceptable traits. In other words, when facing a problem, aim for a solution that is good-enough rather than perfectly optimal, especially when operating under conditions where you lack information. In many ways, satisficing is what most of us do completely unconsciously in everyday human interactions. By communicating we arrive at a consensus that meets a minimum acceptable standard without knowing everything that is influencing the decision; especially all of the feelings of the other people involved. Many outside advisors in succession planning tend to forget that family businesses are created by people, and people are complex, feeling beings that operate from emotions, which come from a set of deeply-rooted past beliefs.

What the process of ascending, and the tool of the Safe Space, do is widen the field of possible information—crucially, emotional information—allowing us to raise the minimum acceptable standard we use to make our decisions. Maintaining the summit is in the discipline of using these tools as much as possible in every area of life, from relationships to business. That way, we are navigating our decision-making with higher resolution—having as much information available to us as we can take in.

When Anton Oliver and the All Blacks were taking stock of their shocking loss against France in 2007, Oliver realized the All Blacks needed to evaluate the old traditions by which the century-old team had operated. By confronting those traditions and identifying which were holding the All Blacks in the vise-grip of a negative emotional tradition, they were able to design new emotional traditions that aligned better with their current reality. A clinical psychologist was brought in to explain the anatomy of the nervous system to the All Blacks; the stress hormone cortisol—present in massive quantities when the nervous system's fight, flight, or freeze response was activated—affected them when they were playing. The All Blacks needed to understand their mental game to fully grasp the mechanics of what was happening to them on the pitch. If any player was feeling fearful, telling himself that he could fail and would never live up the pressures of the legacy he carried, then he would be operating from a state of chronic activation of his fight, flight, or freeze response. How could that not affect his presence on the rugby pitch and his playing ability?

Bringing in a specialist to help you is a critical component of fine tuning. Experts can see into your blind spots. Widening the information field, by bringing an understanding of the biological mechanisms of fight, flight, or freeze going on inside of each player, enabled them to engage in the process of satisficing. Whether he knew it or not, by widening the information field and bringing more data to the discussion, Anton Oliver was acting as a futurist—someone who scans the near horizon and makes predictions that arise from observing present trends and conditions. An interdisciplinary systems-thinking is part of what will become a necessity for you to maintain your position on the summit; you will need to become a futurist.

A Futurism From the Inside

In 1931 as a boiling Monsoon swept away a steel grey sun, an eight-year-old Nirmala pressed the hem of her sari beneath her feet to keep it dry. She stood at the entrance of the college, built by the rough hands of British men with their strange words. Her heart pounded louder than the temple chimes. She turned once, glancing at the fading outline of her mother's shadow down the street. They had argued bitterly that morning—her mother called it betrayal, her father called it treasonous. Nirmala resolved, one day she would study the British; learn what they had learned; master their law, envelop their language in the musical tongue of her own, and use their strange words like a spell—*I will make them leave*, she thought to herself as the monsoon broke, and the streets surrendered to a red torrent of wet dust.

Years later, in 1947, the night had bled into dawn. Nirmala, twenty-four years old, her hands, once burned by British irons, held a tiny paper flag—saffron, white, and green. She didn't wave it. She simply looked at it. Stared at it like a newborn's face. The Blue Union Jack lowering for the last time—without fanfare, without drumroll; a slow, whispering melancholic descent. Nirmala remembered the students—beaten for speaking Hindi in class. She remembered the salt marches, the arrests, the funerals, a sharp tug and a clatter of rope pulleys, the tricolor rose. People cried, shouted, and fell to their knees. India was theirs. India was hers. Behind her, a British officer quietly stepped into a simmering black car, holding a hat. The car lurched away, unnoticed.

Futurism is typically considered a discipline firmly rooted in the exacting world of technology and machines. However, there might be an aspect to futurism as a discipline and practice that contends with the immaterial; what's on the inside, our hearts and minds; how we see ourselves as thinking, feeling creatures and what alignment in those realms can do not only for us as individuals, but for the group. A torrid and distinct nation sprawling the Subcontinent between the Asian landmass and the vast Indian Ocean, India has been inhabited by humans for two million years and is among the oldest continuously inhabited landmasses on Earth. A nation of high deserts and higher mountains, dense jungles and mighty rivers that nourish a vast floodplain which has given rise to nearly 14 distinct human civilizations over 9,000 years. A nation of vast natural beauty and abundant natural wealth, or spiritual enlightenment and ethnic and religious friction. India is a palimpsest in the form of a nation, embodied by layers upon layers of remaking and renewal with a new future horizon constantly on the brink of reshaping its face.

By 1923, India had existed as a colonial possession of the British Empire for 266 years, and having been politically incorporated into the Empire in 1765 and 1858, was directly ruled by Great Britain for 65 years. What resulted was a mélange of ancient and Victorian Emotional Traditions that would ultimately and eternally change the future of both Great Britain and India.

The vast natural and inevitably human resources of India—textiles like silks and linens, tea, and infamously the narcotic drug opium—would fund the Industrial Revolution in Britain, facilitating the need for British naval supremacy and ultimately placing the island nation on the top of the economic heap throughout the 19th century.

India in turn inspired a romantic obsession with the "Orient," in Britain that would explode in architecture (for example, Brighton Pavilion); popular literature, such as the iconic works of Rudyard Kipling; fashion; and especially the institution of tea. The British-built university system would sprout colleges and universities in Calcutta and Bombay, giving birth to a new Indian elite steeped in centuries of English tradition and Western philosophy. While these educated Indian elites were trained to serve the good of the Empire, they would eventually become the unexpected intellectual engine of the Indian independence movement that would deploy England's own liberal and nationalist arguments against British rule, liberating India.

Nirmala Srivastava was born in 1923, in Chhindwara, Madhya Pradesh, in the heart of British colonial India. Her Hindu father, Prasad Salve, was a descendant of the Satavahana royal dynasty and a renowned member of the educated Indian elite. Fluent in 14 languages, Prasad had been the first to translate the Quran into Marathi and was one of the first Indians ever elected to the nation's Central Legislative Assembly. Nirmala's Christian mother, Cornelia Salve, was the first woman in India ever to earn an honors degree in mathematics.

Nirmala's accomplished and cerebrally gifted parents were idealists, and the young girl was immersed in the kinetic discourse of the Indian Independence movement from the age of her first steps as a little girl in Chhindwara, not as a passive observer but a child-participant. Even at her young age, she could see India's independence as necessary "purification" for the ancient nation's future. "The feeling that whatever our parents were doing for the country's freedom was so great—so elevating," said Nirmala looking back on her girlhood, "we didn't think to ask for the comforts that children ask for." Nirmala has been raised in an emotional tradition of self-sacrifice for the greater good; in order for the nation to become truly sovereign, once again able to determine its own destiny on its own terms, each and every individual Indian would first have to become sovereign within themselves. A nation of sovereign individuals could not be ruled by outsiders. Emotional traditions such as this one in which Nirmala had been raised, instilled a tendency toward thinking with the future first. They shift human preoccupation, from surviving the present, to calculating how the present becomes the future, and which present trends might become predominate in that future.

It would be before the age of ten that Nirmala would become a forgotten child in a time of upheaval. When she was eight-years-old, her avant-garde parents were arrested and jailed for agitating against colonial rule. The small girl, on her own initiative, took up the responsibility of caring for her young siblings while her parents were incarcerated. Her ability to do this difficult, demanding and high-responsibility task was built on her preparedness—an innate and cellular understanding of what her siblings—those who like her would have future needs—required in order to remain healthy. Nirmala and her siblings lived a spartan, austere existence, while separated from their imprisoned parents. They were evicted from their affluent home and lived in small huts and slept on the floor. They foraged and scrounged for food, sometimes going hungry, yet they survived.

In 1942, at 19 years old, Nirmala herself would be jailed and tortured for agitating against British colonial rule in India. While attending university at the Science College in Nagpur, she had met Mahatma Ghandi—the anti-colonial nationalist and political ethicist leader of the Indian Independence movement who would be credited for using his philosophy of non-violence defiance to end British colonial rule in India. Nirmala had followed in her parents' footsteps; Gandhi had made her a youth leader at nineteen. And the young woman was warned by a friend of the family that her participation would be very dangerous work for a young woman like her. In response her father intervened and told her, "Don't listen to this man! I'm so very proud of you. I hope all my children become like you."

Five years later, at the stroke of midnight, August 14, 1947, India once again became a free and sovereign nation. The sudden self-determination unleashed an explosion of pent-up angst and frustration as the major nationalist factions within India scrambled to claim power and form a government. Hindus and Muslims were in conflict in the streets as the populations, who had long been kept separate and from fighting amongst each other during British rule, took advantage of the chaos to settle old scores. When riots broke out in the streets of cities all across India, Nirmala—newly married and pregnant with her first child—was sheltering at home when there was a brusque knock at her door.

Hesitatingly she opened it, risking her safety. "When Nirmala opened it," recalled her younger brother, Babamama many years later, "she found one lady and two gentlemen standing at the entrance looking extremely frightened and scared. They told Nirmala that they were refugees from Pakistan and since one of them was a Muslim, the Hindus were after them, chasing them with drawn swords. Nirmala took them in without a moment's hesitation and hid them in a room." Moments later, a band of stern sword-wielding men showed up at her door no doubt hunting for the Muslims she had just agreed to hide. Nirmala opened the door and bluffed them saying she, "was a staunch Hindu herself, so how could she give protection to a Muslim?" The Hindu captain brandished his drawn sword and glared at her, initially in disbelief. But Nirmala, wore a large red *bindi*—the red ritual dot Hindu's mark on the forehead to signal a woman's marriage to a Hindu man. Seeing the bindi, the men softened, sheathed their menacing curved swords and dematerialized back into the riot as quickly as they came.

It was clear to Nirmala that humans could find themselves easily whipped up into a frenzy by the rhetoric of politicians, activists and provocateurs. The entire population of India had been unified against the rule by outsiders and now they were turning on each other. No matter their external reality, or the constant flux of political circumstances, humans would always need a way to find their inner silence and grasp some quantum of self-awareness. Her futurism wasn't thinking merely about the here and now; her futurism was focused on the next Independence movement, in the next nation yearning to break free of colonial rule, and the next frenzy of rioting and persecution that would inevitably ensue. Nirmala was thinking of the human race as something that would outlast her, and future humans—even those completely unlike her—would need a tool to survive their future, no matter what it might bring.

Nirmala would spend the remaining 60 years of her life devoted to developing a system—a new emotional tradition—to enable all humankind to cultivate an inner peace and inner sovereignty. She developed the tradition of Sahaja Yoga—a democratized yogic system of self-realization that could be learned and practiced by anyone. For thousands of years, the teachings of most yoga traditions had been hidden behind a veil of elitism. Nirmala brought a new form of yoga to the masses that put the ability to cultivate an "inner-silence," a quieting of the mind that brings about keen self-awareness, self-realization and personal sovereignty, directly in the hands of everyday people. Her futurism enabled the world to have access to these principles of yoga and apply themselves in the emancipation of humankind.

Living in the Future, Now

While Gandhi's philosophy of *satyagraha*, meaning "holding firmly to the truth as a force"—a set of values that emphasized *ahimsa*, "non-violence" as a kind of anvil that could break all hammers–was foundational of moral futurism that taught and inspired Nirmala, she took Gandhi's principles one step further: She internalized the principle that true and lasting freedom cannot come through applying external force against something, but only through a discipline of self-mastery. It was in this way that she saw the Indian struggle for independence as a national goal that mirrored and depended upon the individual's internal struggle to master the ego, curb violence, and overcome centuries of social conditioning. Her futurism was one built upon, not the technology of humankind, but the internal individual revolution each human being is capable of. That revolution could bring moral clarity where there had previously been a cloud of reactivity and responses conditioned by trauma and rhetoric.

Being a futurist in your family and in your business is to realize that your past is leaking all over your present, impacting your future succession plans. The future of your generational wealth depends on your ability to stop the leak.

Questions to ponder:

1. When you consider the future of your family, what do you see?
2. When you consider the future of your business, what do you predict?
3. What would need to change in order to have a different, more optimal future for your family?
4. What would need to change in order to have a different, more optimal future for your business?

CHAPTER 17

The Savage Mountain

In 1941, in the North Pacific, 230 miles north of Oahu, the glimmering deck of the Imperial Japanese aircraft carrier *Akagi* was slick with sea mist; the thrum of growling airplane engines, a thunder in the steel lap of *Akagi*. Strapped into his cockpit, Shigeharu Murata's gloved hands clasped a tiny inro, worn smooth, lacquered black with fine gold cranes etched along the lid—a gift from his mother on the day he earned his commission. Inside the inro was a scrap of yellowed washi paper; a brushstroke poem he had written years earlier, "steel under heaven, honor without return, silent wind names the departed." Shigeharu recited the prayer his mother had taught him, "May my ancestors regard me. May the Emperor be proud."

The radio crackled his awareness snapping back to the present. Admiral Nagumo's voice, stoic and unshaken "Climb Mount Niitaka." The final order. Proceed with attack.

Shigeharu's cockpit trembled with the force of the steam catapult, vaulting his Nakajima B5N "Kate" torpedo bomber into the sea-sprayed air of the Pacific. Below, *Akagi* dematerialized in the mist. Ahead, beyond the sun-drenched horizon, lay the sleeping American.

Yamamoto's gamble was now in motion—beyond remorse, beyond return; 183 aircraft reaching South and East. Torpedo bombers. Dive bombers. Zeros—the mostly wooden fighter aircraft made by Mitsubishi. The Rising Sun of Japan painted bold and red on each wing, glistening like fresh blood in the morning light. Ahead, the ink-dark sea rolled. Beyond it, Pearl Harbor slept—unaware.

The Sunday of December 7, 1941 began as any other December Sunday morning in Oahu. A wet sun yawned over the harbor. The water lay still, glassy, dotted with American battleships. The USS *Arizona*, *Oklahoma*, *California*, and many others at anchor around the flat knoll of Ford Island, gleamed in the morning light. Sailors lingered on deck, coffee in hand. A few hovered around a workhorse radio tuned to swing. Others reposed below deck, slung in hammocks, dreaming of girls and home. In the mess, men lined up for breakfast. Eggs. Sausages.

On the mainland, birds wheeled above the groggy harbor. Church bells reverberated in the distant hills. A couple stood on the shore, pointing at what looked like a strange flock of sea birds in tight formation. And then—a hum. The deep, distant hum that wasn't birds, or wind. It grew, a crescendo screaming of metal on air; the unnatural wail drawn up from the depths of someone's nightmare. Fire and blackened steel bloomed from the Arizona's magazine in a roar that split the sea. Men ran shouting into oily pitch-dark smoke, leaping from the decks into water thick with flame and death. Machine gun crews scrambled barefoot to stations, returning fire too late. Torpedoes slashed beneath the surface, tearing open the belly of *Arizona*. The sky over Oahu, only moments before blue and soft, now in an instant seethed with flame.

When 353 Imperial Japanese aircraft screamed down out of the sun, the Americans were completely stunned and utterly vulnerable. More than 180 U.S. aircrafts were destroyed, 4 battleships sunk, another 4 crippled, 1,178 Americans were wounded, and 2,403 were killed. The next day, the United States formally declared war on the Empire of Japan and entered World War II. And in that infamous rupture, one era ended and another began.

Succession in life is Emotional, Not Tactical.

There's no preparing for the unknown. We cannot predict the future. All we can do is prepare ourselves for the possibilities to come and when they eventually arise we can meet those external challenges with the resources, system and processes we have available. Whether in business or in life, preparedness, as we've discussed, encompasses intellectual, practical, experiential and emotional dimensions. The United States of 1941 was not the military and technological powerhouse it is today. The nation had only just emerged from the crush of a Great Depression which had crippled industries and dimmed the future of a generation.

The Japanese bombing of Pearl Harbor, had caught the sleeping industrial giant of the United States of America completely by surprise. Although the Empire of Japan had been waging war in Asia since 1931 when Imperial Japanese forces had invaded and annexed the Chinese state of Manchuria, remaking it into the vassal state of Manchukuo and installing the Chinese emperor Puyi—who had been deposed by his own people—to rule the new puppet state, American attitudes towards a rapidly destabilizing world were largely marked by isolationism and non-intervention.

Japan was rising. A new emotional tradition of regional supremacy and sovereign economic dominance had begun to transform the ancient and once-feudal nation into an industrial contender. And with industry comes hunger. The Imperial Japanese military's ability to project power across East Asia required resources. By 1937, full-scale war had erupted in China, culminating with Imperial Japanese forces condemning 200,000 to 340,000 Chinese civilians, many of them women and children to wholesale brutality and death in the Chinese city of Nanjing.

In response to the atrocity, the United States cut off vital oil exports to Japan. By 1941, The British Empire and the Dutch East Indies had followed suit.

For Japan, this embargo on vital resources for its territorial expansion machine was an existential threat. Under their current operating conditions, Japan's military and civilian industries had only a meagre two-year supply of oil reserves left. Complete exhaustion of the oil reserves would eventually lead to chaos; civil unrest and national upheaval would quickly engulf the island nation consuming everything in its path. Japanese leadership felt the dire need to act. With only two years of oil reserve remaining, only a singular decisive action to knock out the Americans' ability to police the North Pacific, would allow Japan to consolidate her empire and find her vital oil reserves elsewhere. For Japanese leadership, committing to this course of action was neither fully strategic, nor tactical. It was an emotional decision built on one existential necessity: *strike, or perish.*

The Japanese people, inculcated into an emotional tradition of Japan's existential manifest destiny in the Pacific and in the emotional tradition of supreme loyalty to Emperor Hirohito, were emotionally prepared to risk awakening a sleeping American giant in order to secure their legacy. The Americans were emotionally prepared to expend countless lives on far-flung slivers of sand no one at home had ever heard of, in order to end the war in the Pacific.

Being prepared for what may come is emotional, not tactical.

The intellectual, practical and experiential dimensions of our preparedness require us to ask ourselves, "Do I know what to do and how to do it?" The emotional dimension entreats us to ask, "Can I bear to do it?" and "Do I have what it takes?" Without undertaking The Ascent, there can't be an answer to that question backed by any empirical evidence. We could gaslight ourselves into the belief that we can take on and overcome anything because of what we have previously overcome, achieved or built. Yet, those accomplishments, while important and substantial, likely happened while we were operating deep within the skin of the impostor. For many of us, some of those achievements arose while we were meeting our human needs in unhealthy ways. Those internal patterns—our Beasts of Burden—are liabilities when we make them about serving our unmet needs. They could become assets when we make them about nurturing our relationships with others. As the impostor, our need for certainty might have shown up as control. Made about others, our need for certainty could be met in how we create certainty for others by fine tuning how we show up. As the impostor, our need for variety might show up as excessive risk-taking or self-sabotaging behaviors. Made about others, our need for variety could be satisfied by openness to connection with others who we may have previously overlooked. As the impostor, our need for Significance and to make a contribution could show up as a craving for attention. Made about others, our need for significance might be transformed into how we create opportunities to do significant things in the world in ways that include our family. Each and every one of our human needs has a dimension that can be met by great acts of service and inclusion.

In the great challenges of history and in succession, many people have often known what must be done but struggle to act—because the emotional cost is high. **Emotional preparedness is the invisible architecture that supports decisive, timely action under pressure** and it is the greatest gift that parents and leaders can bestow on those who come after them. The knowledge of skills and logistics and tactics will only get you so far. Knowing that you have the emotional self-awareness and emotional clarity to act intentionally, with a designed Emotional Tradition is what allows you to design and build a lasting emotional legacy.

The final lesson comes from the highest mountains on Earth.

Towering at 8,611 meters (28,251 ft) in the Karakoram range, above Pakistan-administered Kashmir, K2 is one of the deadliest mountains on Earth. Roughly 1 in 4 climbers who attempt K2's summit are never seen again. By contrast, Everest, due to decades of support infrastructure, now has a fatality rate below 1 percent. Without high-altitude rescue helicopters, or Sherpas setting up placed ropes in advance, climbers on K2 must be completely self-reliant, able to make quick and correct decisions in chronically lethal conditions; a climber on K2 is his or her own safety system.

The second highest in the world, K2 is a harrowing vertical gauntlet of advanced alpine climbing: steep faces, narrow ridgelines, mixed ice and rock sections, and unstable snowfields. There's no easy route on K2. Every approach, even the popular South Col, are infamous and dangerous, and weather windows are rare and fleeting temptations as if offered up by a trickster spirit to the overconfident and ill-prepared. While Everest is the tallest mountain in the world at 8,848 meters (29,029 ft), K2 is known as the King of Mountains, not because of its towering height but because its faces are significantly more technical than Everest's.

Why would the best climbers on the planet want to summit K2 and not Everest? Because the hardest and most demanding challenges are what will make you better. On your ascent you've stopped wandering in the repeating circles that make up the Land of Familiar on the Valley Floor; you've proceeded towards the challenge of the mountain's face, embracing the danger of unknown hazards. You've confronted the stories you tell yourself about yourself, traversed the icefields of your family's entrenched emotional traditions and anchored your ascent with new ones. You've gained the support of other climbers along the way, working collaboratively and as a team through structured dialogue to design a route to the summit; you've gained the summit, and you've maintained your place there at a dizzying height above the clouds.

The summit is not a sanctuary; it is a moment. From the peak you can see there's even more mountain around the next corner. And then there's even more mountain after that; the shining wall of Gasherbrum and its majestic glacier; "little" Annapurna at a mere 7,219 meters (23,684 feet). That mountain's avalanches are among the deadliest in the world and the naked face of Nanga Parbat, the dramatic "Killer Mountain", stands vertical and unforgiving over Pakistan's meadows. There are as many ascents in the world as there are mountains, each of them offering their own unique challenges, hazards and conditions and just when you think you're good enough, you might have to get better. You can never truly reach the top; there's always a place to go next.

The summit doesn't erase the version of you that climbed it; it offers only a vantage point. The next path could be even more treacherous because you carry the illusion of completion but now you can read the terrain, choose the best holds, and have others on the path to anchor you. That's the essence of The Ascent—not blindly charging toward the next peak, hungry for dopamine or the rush of adrenaline but into the crucial, timeless work of *becoming*.

Meeting the challenges that inevitably arise along the way requires that you understand not just your business and ownership path, but to get a clear view of your family's emotional traditions. Your relationship with yourself will be different. Your relationships with your family members will be different, and your family's emotional future will be different. This different alignment will enable you to design a better self, better relationships and ultimately a better life. And even more importantly, you'll give your family the gift of a rich emotional legacy. And that is the most valuable currency of all.

Conclusion

We start the journey together with a question: "What is an emotional legacy?"

Now that you have come to the end, my hope is that you have now been able to not just understand the connection emotional traditions play in wealth transfer planning, you have given serious thought and hopefully been inspired to want to create your own emotional legacy for generations to come.

My hope is that you dare to be great and break the chains of the past emotional traditions that were handed down to you and do not serve you or your family. As you know you will be contributing to creating an emotionally safer world for yourself, your family and the future generations to come. You will have left the jersey in a much better place.

I am going to give you the formula to ensure you make this happen for yourself and your family.

It starts with having a crystal-clear vision for your family and financial wealth; these must be inseparable and must be designed to support, protect and strengthen the other.

The second part involves addressing all the issues both financially, emotionally and relationally that could get in the way of the vision. This requires a deep dive and the courage to be honest with yourself and each other.

Next is about creating an environment of Emotional Safety (Safe Space) for you as an individual and then collectively as a family.

Finally, designing a platform/process to ensure you maintain the Safe Space across generations, to be able to address issues and ensure the vision is achieved and honored.

This is the journey from the valley floor to base camp and the summit. The joy, the sense of fulfillment and achievement come from maintaining your summit and being the highest version of yourself.

I want to thank you for joining me, and for your curiosity and desire to leave this place in a much different place than where you found it.

With love and gratitude.
Francesco
December 2025

About the Author

For more than twenty years, Francesco Lombardo has been a family business advisor to some of the world's most successful and affluent families. His early years spent in the corporate world, in tandem with his own journey of emotional self-discovery, gave Franco a deep insight into the unique pressures facing high-net-worth families and the complexity of not only sustaining their financial wealth, but their emotional wealth. It was these observations that inspired Franco to set up Veritage, his coaching and advisory firm for wealth-owning families, that exclusively focuses on emotional governance.

As a leading global expert on the emotional impact money and wealth has on relationships within family businesses, he is committed to assisting families find, create, and maintain emotional safety by developing new models for cultural governance, which contributes to the stability, continuity and sustainability of the family business enterprise, its wealth and its legacy.

Franco is an avid rugby fan and loves nothing more than sharing a good bottle of wine with friends and family.

www.ingramcontent.com/pod-product-compliance
Lightning Source LLC
LaVergne TN
LVHW091126080826
845145LV00008B/2055